Brain Facts

Brain Development

Brain Disorders

Brain Facts

Cells of the Nervous System

The Forebrain

The Hindbrain

Learning and Memory

Meditation and Hypnosis

The Midbrain

The Neurobiology of Addiction

Pain

Sleep and Dreaming

Speech and Language

The Spinal Cord

Brain Facts

Louis Vera-Portocarrero, Ph.D.

Series Editor
Eric H. Chudler, Ph.D.

Brain Facts

Chelsea House
An imprint of Infobase Publishing
132 West 31st Street
New York, NY 10001

Library of Congress Cataloging-in-Publication Data

Vera-Portocarrero, Louis.
Brain facts / Louis Vera-Portocarrero.
p. cm.—(Gray matter)
Includes bibliographical references and index.
ISBN 0-7910-8956-8 (hardcover)
1. Brain—Juvenile literature. I. Title. II. Series.
QP376.V47 2006
612.8'2—dc22 2006014243

Chelsea House books are available at special discounts when purchased in bulk quantities for businesses, associations, institutions, or sales promotions. Please call our Special Sales Department in New York at (212) 967-8800 or (800) 322-8755.

You can find Chelsea House on the World Wide Web at http://www.chelseahouse.com

Series and cover design by Terry Mallon

Printed in the United States of America

Bang EJB 10 9 8 7 6 5 4 3 2 1

This book is printed on acid-free paper.

All links and Web addresses were checked and verified to be correct at the time of publication. Because of the dynamic nature of the Web, some addresses and links may have changed since publication and may no longer be valid.

Contents

1 Facts About Neurons

The human nervous system is divided into the central nervous system (CNS), which includes the brain and spinal cord, and the peripheral nervous system (PNS), which includes the cranial nerves, arising from the brain, and the spinal nerves, arising from the spinal cord. The basic functional units in our nervous system are the nerve cells (neurons) and glial cells (glia). There are about 100 billion neurons in the human brain. Neurons present a great variety of sizes and shapes. Most of them possess a long process called the **axon** and a main body known as the cell body or **soma.** Neurons also possess a series of smaller processes called **dendrites** (Figure 1.1). The principal function of the neuron is to communicate information. The dendrites of the neurons receive information from other neurons, and this information is passed to the soma, where the information can be modified and then passed along to other neurons via the axon.

The size of neurons varies, ranging from 5 micrometers (μm) to 100 μm in diameter. Many axons are short, only a millimeter (0.039 inches) in length, but some, like those that extend from the cerebral cortex to the spinal cord, measure a meter (39.37 inches) or more. To gain a sense of the relative size of the neurons, we can examine the neurons that control our muscle movements, which are called **motor neurons.** These neurons have their cell bodies in the spinal cord and

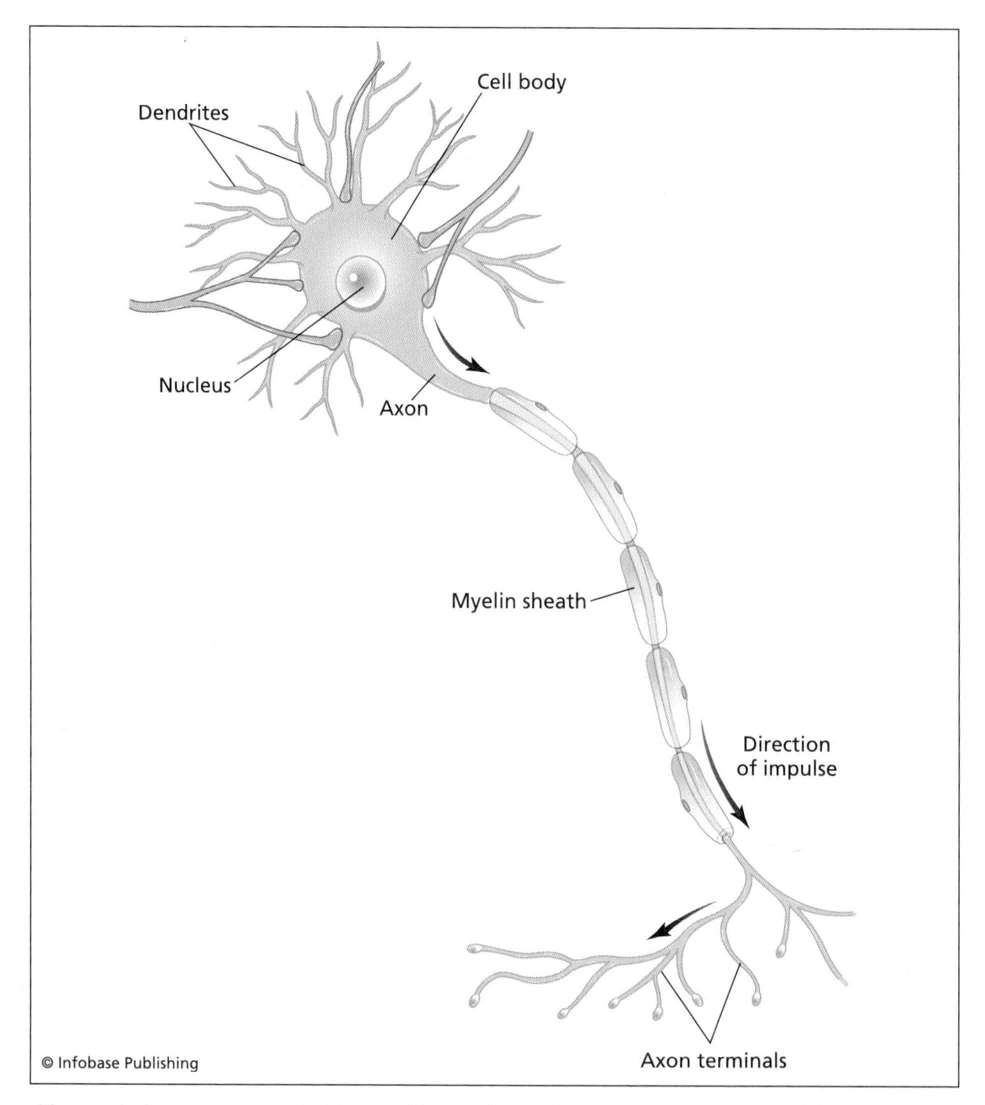

Figure 1.1 The neuron is the building block of the nervous system. Neurons have specialized features, such as dendrites and axons, that allow them to communicate using a combination of electrical and chemical signals.

send their axons to the different muscles to exert their control. The motor neurons that control our leg muscles are some of the longest in the nervous system, extending from the spinal

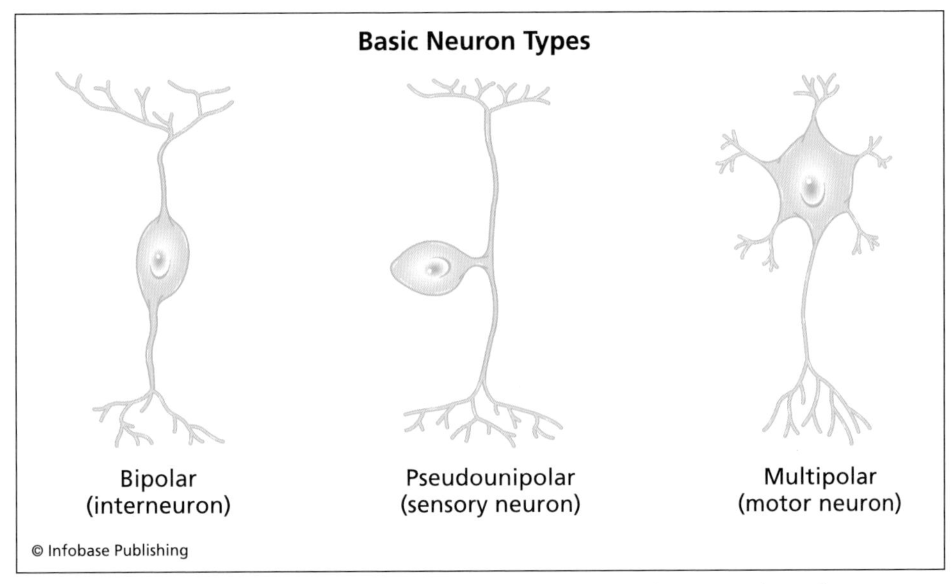

Figure 1.2 Neurons can be classified by their shape and the number of processes (dendrites or axons) that extend from the cell body. Each type of neuron has a different role within the nervous system.

cord through the length of the lower extremities. If we were to imagine the soma of a spinal motor neuron as being the size of a tennis ball, then its dendrites would spread out through a room-sized volume, and its axon would correspond to a half-inch garden hose nearly half a mile long.

CLASSIFICATION OF NEURONS

Neurons may be classified according to their structure or function. The functional classification is based on the direction that neurons conduct impulses. **Sensory** or **afferent** neurons conduct impulses from sensory receptors into the nervous system. **Motor** or **efferent** neurons conduct impulses out of the nervous system to different organs (muscles, glands, etc.). Association neurons or **interneurons** are located within the CNS and serve the integrative functions of the nervous system.

There are two types of motor neurons: **somatic** and **autonomic**. Somatic motor neurons provide both reflex and voluntary control of muscles. Autonomic motor neurons innervate the involuntary organs: gut, heart muscle, glands and blood vessels. The autonomic motor neurons are the basic units of the autonomic nervous system, which will be discussed in Chapter 5.

The structural classification of neurons is based on the number of processes that extend from the cell body of the neuron (Figure 1.2). **Bipolar neurons** have two processes, one at each end; this type is found in the retina of the eye. **Multipolar neurons** have several dendrites and one axon extending from the cell body; this is the most common type of neuron. A **pseudounipolar neuron** has a single short process that divides like a T to form a longer process. Sensory neurons are pseudounipolar; one end of the process formed by the T receives sensory stimuli and produces nerve impulses, and the other end of the T delivers these impulses to neurons within the brain or spinal cord.

NEUROGLIA

The neuroglia, or glial cells, are the supportive cells in the nervous system. There are six types of glial cells. One of the main functions of glial cells is to provide a physical framework for the neurons in the nervous system. The glial cells accomplish this by producing a substance called **myelin.** In the PNS, a type of glial cell known as a Schwann cell forms a myelin sheath surrounding the axons of neurons. In the CNS, oligodendrocytes are the glial cells responsible for this formation. The myelin sheath enables electrical impulses to travel at faster rates than without the presence of myelin along the length of the axon. In the PNS, the myelin sheath allows for nerve regeneration.

Table 1.1 Types of Glial Cells

NEUROGLIA	FUNCTIONS
Schwann cells	Surround axon at all peripheral nerve fibers, forming a wrap (myelin sheaths) around fibers in the PNS
Oligodendrocytes	Form myelin sheaths around axons in the CNS
Astocytes	Cover capillaries within brain to help form the blood-brain barrier
Microglia	Cells in the CNS that comprise the immune defense of the nervous system
Ependyma	Lining of brain cavities, produces cerebrospinal fluid

Blood-Brain Barrier

Blood capillaries in the brain, unlike those of most other organs, do not have pores in their walls. Instead, the cells lining the capillaries are joined together by **tight junctions**. These junctions impede the passage of molecules from the bloodstream into the brain tissue. Molecules that do not cross the blood-brain barrier must be moved by different processes. This allows for protection and maintenance of the delicate nervous tissue environment. Nevertheless, the blood-brain barrier presents difficulties in the therapy of brain diseases because drugs that can enter other organs may not be able to enter the brain.

Drugs taken orally reach the bloodstream by being absorbed through the stomach or small intestine. A drug has to cross the capillary wall that separates the brain tissue and the bloodstream to have an effect on the brain. If drugs that are destined for the brain will not cross this barrier, they must be injected directly into the cerebrospinal fluid or into the brain tissue itself. Many pharmaceutical companies today expend millions of dollars doing research to design new drugs that are small enough to cross the blood-brain barrier and exert effects on the CNS. Some of the molecules that these companies produce are lipid (fat) soluble so they will be able to diffuse through the blood-brain barrier, since the barrier is made up of lipids.

Regeneration of a Cut Axon

Neurons in the peripheral nervous system have the capacity to withstand and recover from a certain degree of injury. After a nerve fiber is crushed or severed, both central and peripheral portions undergo changes. The distal or peripheral portion degenerates. This occurs because the axon receives its sustenance from the neuronal cell body. This degeneration is called Wallerian degeneration. After a period of one week, from the central end (the end closest to the cell body), the divided fiber starts to grow at a rate of 1 to 2 millimeters per day. Numerous sprouts or branches grow across scar tissue at the injury site toward the original site of termination. Even a severed major nerve may be surgically reconnected and the function of the nerve largely reestablished if the surgery is performed before tissue death. However, many axons may reach a termination that is inappropriate and others are lost in the scar tissue. This process is responsible for possible complications that can produce chronic pain. In the central nervous system, axons have a much more limited ability to regenerate than peripheral axons.

TRANSMISSION OF INFORMATION IN THE NERVOUS SYSTEM

The nervous system transmits information using electrical impulses. These electrical impulses are generated in the cell membrane. The cell membrane contains specific channels that allow for the passage of sodium ions into the cell and potassium ions out of the cell, which produces an **electrical potential** across the membrane called the resting membrane potential. In this resting potential, the inside of the cell is negatively charged in comparison to the outside of the cell. This potential difference is largely the result of the permeability properties of the cell membrane. An increase in membrane permeability to a specific ion results in the diffusion of that ion down its concentration gradient, either into or out of the cell. When an electrical stimulus is applied, the membrane responds with changes in ion permeabilities. The membrane allows the entrance of sodium ions, which makes the inside of the cell more positive. After a period of time, potassium ions start to diffuse out of the cell. Since potassium is positively charged, the diffusion of potassium out of the cell makes the inside less positive and acts to restore the original membrane potential. The rapid diffusion of sodium ions into the cell and the consequent exit of potassium ions produce the **action potential** or nerve impulse.

When an action potential is produced, it occurs at a small section of the axonal membrane (where the ion channels are located). For about the first millisecond of the action potential, a current of sodium ions enters the cell at that patch of membrane. These positively charged sodium ions are conducted by the cable properties of the axon to an adjacent region of axonal membrane that still has a resting membrane potential. This helps the next patch of membrane to become depolarized and it too produces another action potential, which then travels down the axon.

Brain Imaging

How do we visualize brain activity? Brain imaging has existed for the last three decades and it enables us to look at the brain anatomy and its areas of activation after certain tasks. The modern era of brain imaging began with the development of the computerized tomography (CT) scan. This technique takes advantage of the fact that X-rays reflect the relative density of the tissue through which they pass. Since areas rich in cells and areas rich in axons will have different densities, the CT scan can record the conformations of tissue. In a standard two-dimensional X-ray, such as that used to assess bone fractures, the different brain structures are overlapping and are under very dense bone (the skull). Therefore, it is difficult to visualize individual brain structures. If you pass narrow X-rays though the same object at many different angles, as is done in a CT scan, it is possible to use computing and mathematical techniques to create a visual image of the brain.

Two more advanced techniques were developed after the CT scan. Positron emission tomography (PET) detects positrons emitted by the brain tissue instead of passing X-rays through the tissue. Positrons can be introduced into the brain by having subjects ingest glucose that contains short-acting radioactive atoms. The glucose is transported by the blood to the brain. The idea is that areas of the brain that are active will use more glucose, and hence become more radioactive. The second imaging development from CT scans is magnetic resonance imaging (MRI). MRI is based on the principle that hydrogen atoms behave like spinning magnets in the presence of a magnetic field. Blood flowing though the vessels in the brain move oxygen atoms. This movement can be detected by an MRI magnet. MRI can detect the changes in blood flow induced by brain activity, a procedure called functional MRI (fMRI).

MYELIN

Myelin is a collection of lipid fats and proteins that wraps around the axons of neurons. Myelin increases the speed of nerve signals as they move down the axon. For example, a thin myelinated axon transmits impulses at 5 to 30 meters per second (16 to 100 feet per second), whereas an unmyelinated one transmits them at 0.5 to 2 meters per second (1.6 to 6.5 feet per second). Myelin speeds up the rate of conduction of the nerve. In nerve fibers without myelin, impulses move along in "waves," but in myelinated fiber they hop along the nerve fiber in a process known as saltatory conduction. The myelin sheath provides insulation for the axon, preventing movements of sodium and potassium ions through the membrane. There are interruptions in the myelin sheath called the **nodes of Ranvier.** It is in these nodes where there is a high concentration of sodium channels and where the action potentials occur. Myelin is produced by specialized cells: oligodendrocytes in the CNS, and Schwann cells in the PNS. There are several diseases that affect the myelin, and therefore the impulses of nerve cells, causing nervous system dysfunction. One of the most recognized diseases is multiple sclerosis (MS). Multiple sclerosis is a disease characterized by multiple areas of damage and scarring to the nerve fibers of the CNS (Figure 1.3). The symptoms related to MS are impaired sensation, inability to control or properly move the arms and legs, and changes in vision. As the disease progresses, patients must walk with a cane or be confined to a wheelchair, unable to perform simple day-to-day tasks.

SYNAPSES

The areas where axons meet another cell are called **synapses.** The synapse is the functional connection between a neuron and a second cell. In the CNS, this second cell is also a neuron. In the PNS, the other cell may be a neuron or an effector cell within either a muscle or gland. There are two types of synapses: electrical and

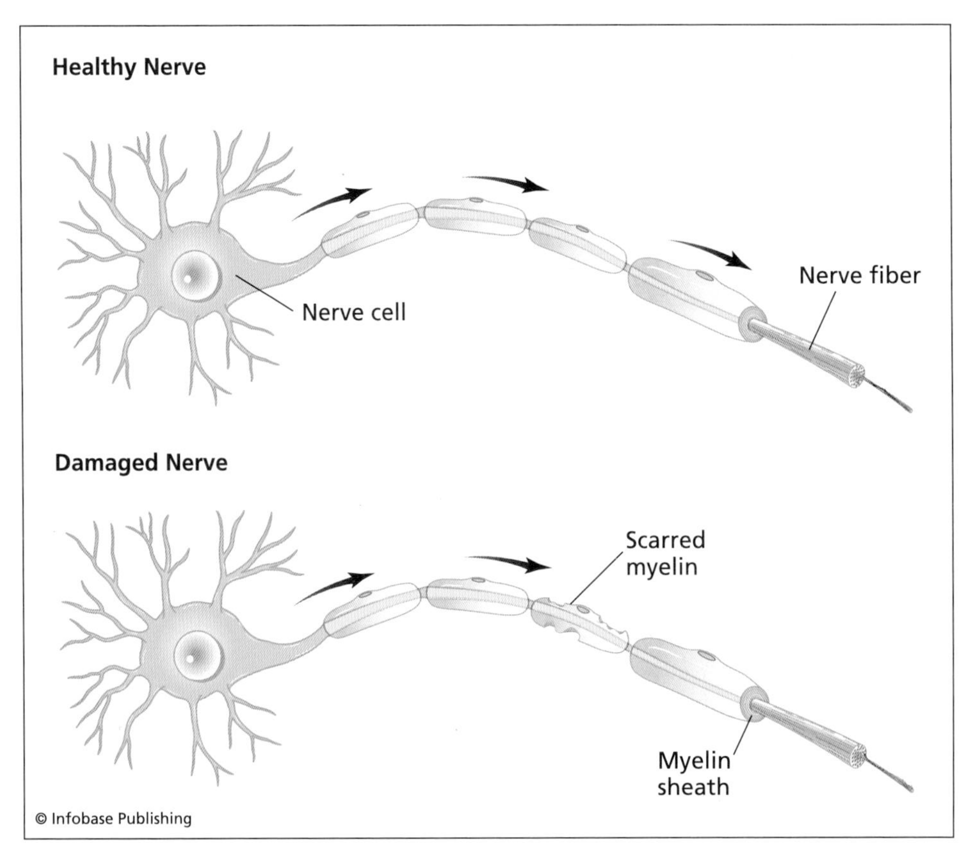

Figure 1.3 The myelin sheath that wraps the axon of a neuron is necessary for speedy transmission of electrical signals. When the myelin is damaged, the nerve cell impulses can be delayed or restricted. Multiple sclerosis is a disease caused by the gradual destruction of myelin.

chemical. Electrical synapses are the electrical coupling of two cells that are approximately equal in size and joined by an area of contact with low electrical resistance. In this way, impulses can be regenerated from one cell to the next without interruption; these areas of contact are called gap junctions. These gap junctions are present in smooth muscle and cardiac muscle where they allow excitation and rhythmic contraction of large masses of muscle cells. Gap junctions have also been observed in various regions of the brain. Although their functional significance here is unknown, it has been speculated that they may allow a two-way transmission of impulses (in contrast to chemical synapses, which are always one way).

Transmission across the majority of synapses in the nervous system is one way and occurs though the release of chemical **neurotransmitters** from presynaptic axon endings. These endings, called axon terminals, are separated from the postsynaptic cell by a synaptic cleft. Neurotransmitter molecules within the terminals are contained within many small synaptic vesicles. In order for the neurotransmitter to be released into the synaptic cleft, the vesicle must fuse with the plasma membrane and release its contents. The neurotransmitter is released following electrical excitation of the axon terminal. There is an inflow of calcium ions into the terminal, which is required for the release of the neurotransmitter. The neurotransmitter then travels through the synaptic cleft and binds to receptors in the postsynaptic cell.

■ **Learn more about neurons** Search the Internet for *synapse, neurotransmitter, action potential, axon,* and *dendrite.*

2 Facts About Brain Development

We rely on our nervous system to interact with our environment. Our nervous system is specialized to handle a myriad of tasks at the same time. This specialization starts during the time of embryonic development and it only stops at the time of death.

DEVELOPMENT OF THE BRAIN

The first indication of nervous tissue development occurs about 17 days following conception, when a thickening appears along the entire **dorsal** length of the embryo. This thickening is called the neural plate, which differentiates to give rise to all of the neurons and to most glial cells. Shortly thereafter, the neural plate begins to fold inward, forming a longitudinal neural groove in the midline, flanked by a parallel neural fold on each side. The neural groove deepens, and the neural folds approach each other in the midline. At the end of the third week after conception, the folds begin to fuse midway to form the **neural tube** (Figure 2.1). This neural tube is the beginning of the brain and spinal cord. For a period of time the ends of the neural tube are open, but they close after the fourth week. Sometimes the tube does not close, leading to certain birth defects. From the neural folds, the **neural crest** forms, which gives rise to the peripheral nervous system (cranial and spinal nerves).

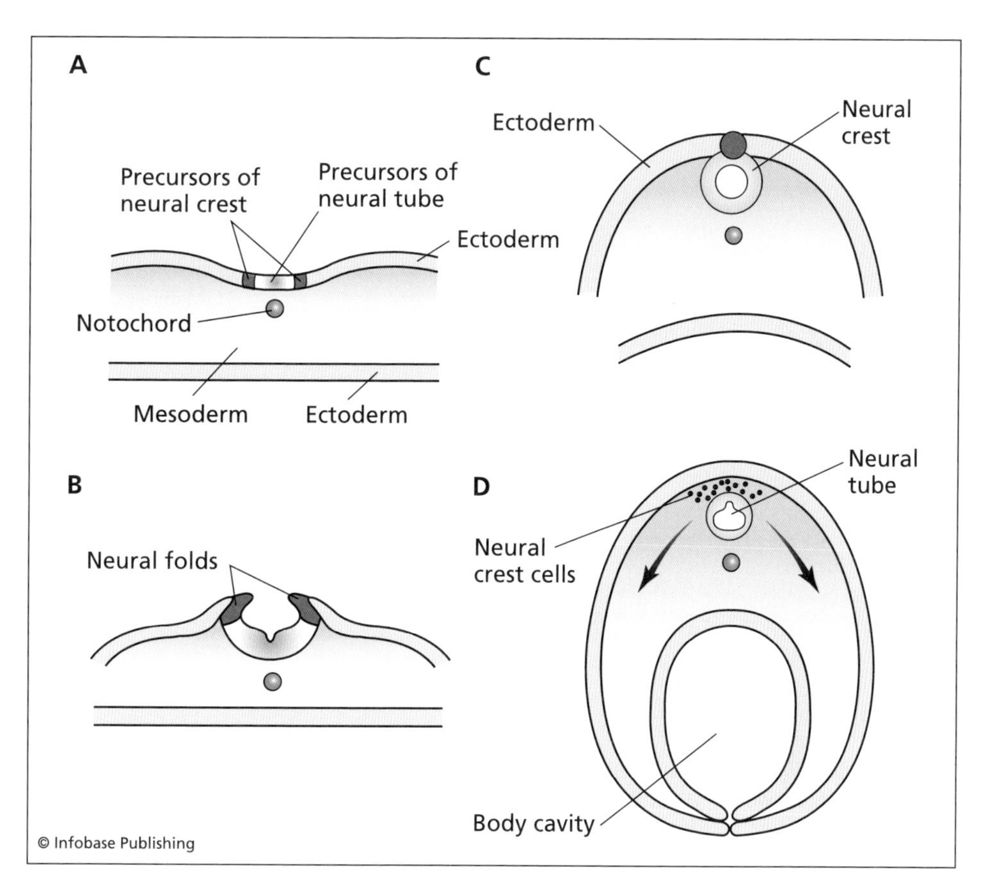

Figure 2.1 In the early embryo, the first step in the development of the nervous system is the formation of the neural plate (A). Once the neural plate is formed, it begins to slowly fold inward (B), and the ends come together to form the neural tube (C), which is the precursor of the brain and spinal cord. Neural crest cells then diffuse (D) to other parts of the embryo to form neurons and various body structures.

The neural tube has a cavity at its center that is conserved throughout development. This cavity develops into the ventricular system of the brain and the central canal of the spinal cord by which cerebrospinal fluid (CSF) travels and bathes all of the central nervous system.

Later during development, the neural tube develops five different swellings that become the main divisions of the brain

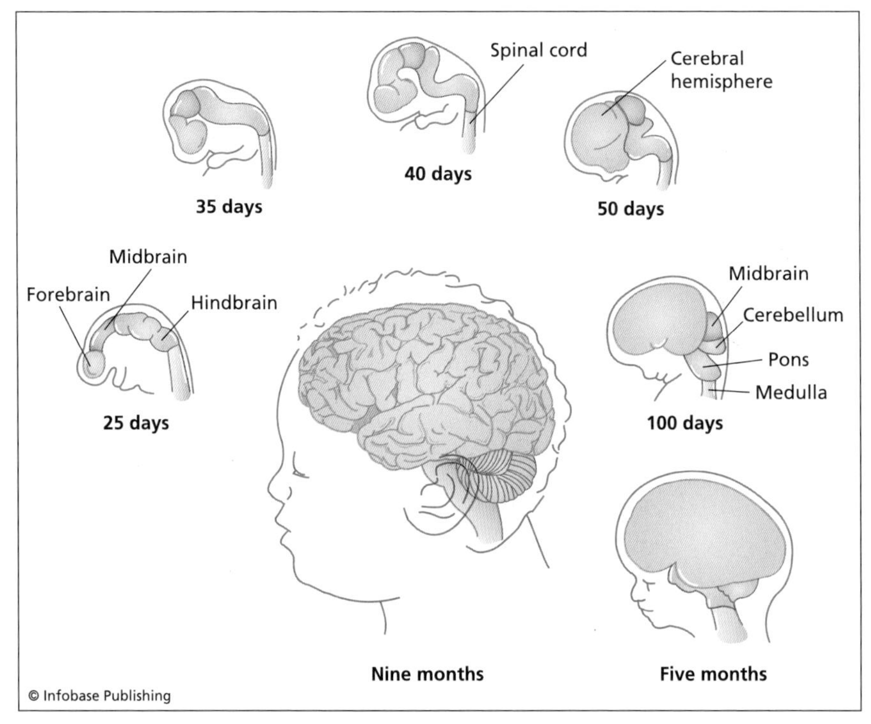

Figure 2.2 This illustration shows the progression of brain growth from four weeks after conception to birth.

(Figure 2.2). These divisions are the **telencephalon** (cerebral cortex), **diencephalon** (forebrain structures such as the thalamus), **mesencephalon** (midbrain), **metencephalon** (pons and cerebellum), and **myelencephalon** (medulla).

DEVELOPMENT OF THE SPINAL CORD

The spinal cord, like the brain, develops as the neural tube undergoes differentiation and specialization. Throughout the developmental process, the hollow central canal persists while the specialized **white** and **gray matter** forms. Changes in the neural tube become apparent during the sixth week as the **lateral** walls thicken to form a groove, called the sulcus limitans, along each lateral wall of the central canal. A pair of alar plates form above the sulcus limitans, and a pair of basal plates forms below it. By the ninth week, the alar plates have specialized to become the dorsal horns, containing fibers of the afferent cell bodies, and the basal plates have specialized to form the **ventral** and lateral horns, containing motor cell bodies.

Developmental Problems

Congenital malformations of the central nervous system are common and frequently involve overlying bone, muscle, and connective tissue. The most severe abnormalities make life impossible, and the less severe malformations frequently result in functional disability. Most congenital malformations occur during the embryonic period. Failure of the neural tube to close can produce malformations. Failure of the cranial (head) portion of the neural tube produces anencephaly, which prevents development of the cerebral hemispheres and the skull, resulting in an undifferentiated mass instead of the normal cranium. The newborn cannot survive. Failure of the rear end of the neural tube to close causes spina bifida. The severity of this malformation varies, and many times the newborn survives when the defect does not involve the spinal cord. When it does, it appears as a saclike protrusion of skin and underlying nervous tissue in the lower back. The amount of nervous tissue involved determines the severity of impairment. Other common congenital problems are malformations of the skull, which do not allow for continuous flow of the cerebrospinal fluid through the ventricular system. This results in hydrocephalus, which is characterized by a large head and soft skull tissue. Many infants born this way either die shortly after or survive with severe cognitive deficits.

Cell Migration

Cell migration is the driving force of development of the brain and spinal cord. Nerve cells form by division in the inner, or ventricular, lining of the brain. Here, each cell gives rise to two daughter cells that either migrate or undergo further division. The division of germinal (stem) cells may be complete by the middle of gestation, whereas the migration of cells to various regions may continue for a number of months, even postnatally (after birth). The mechanisms that control migration and determine the destination of migrating cells are not well understood. It is known that specialized filaments provide a pathway for the migrating cells to follow. Once a group of cells has arrived at the surface of the brain, differentiation (the formation of axons, dendrites, and so on) begins. Subsequently, a new group of cells migrates from the inner lining through the layers already present to form a new outer layer. Thus, a structure such as the cerebral cortex matures from its inner to its outer surface.

AXONS AND DENDRITES

Axons begin sprouting from neurons as they migrate to their targets. The axon grows at a rate of up to 170 microns (0.0067 inches) per hour. Axons have specific targets that they must reach if the neuron is to survive and become functional. The formation of appropriate neural pathways can be disrupted in any number of ways. Axons may be unable to reach their target if their way is blocked, as can happen following scarring from head trauma during the early months of life. The development of axons can also be disrupted by ingestion of toxic substances, malnutrition, or some other disturbance. It can also be disrupted if the axons' target is damaged, in which case the axonal system may degenerate or may occupy an inappropriate target. Should the latter event occur, the behavior supported by the invaded area may also be disrupted.

Dendritic growth usually starts after the cell reaches its final position, and it proceeds at a relatively slow rate. The growth of dendrites parallels that of axons. Generally, the growth of dendrites is timed to intercept corresponding axons. Although dendritic development begins prenatally in humans, it continues for a long time postnatally. Before birth, there are few spines on dendrites, but after birth the spines begin to develop and cover the maturing dendrites densely.

SYNAPTIC FORMATION AND MYELINATION

It is clear from many studies that a given brain region sends axons to a limited number of other regions and that synapses are made only in a specific part of certain cells in that region. The location of synapses is determined by genetic instructions, by the orientation of the cell when the axon arrives, by the timing of axon arrival, and by the use the axons are given once a connection is made. Malfunctions in any of these features of synaptic formation may cause abnormal brain development.

Myelination is the process by which the support cells of the nervous system begin to surround axons and provide them with insulation. Although nerves can become functional before myelination, it is assumed that they reach adult functional levels as myelination is completed. Thus, myelination provides an index of the maturity of structures from which and to which axons project. Myelination begins shortly after birth and continues to increase beyond 15 years of age, and may increase in density as late as age 60.

DEVELOPMENT OF THE PERIPHERAL NERVOUS SYSTEM

Development of the peripheral nervous system produces the pattern of dermatomes within the body. A dermatome is an area of skin **innervated** by the neurons of a certain spinal or cranial nerve. Most of the scalp and face is innervated by sensory neurons from the trigeminal nerve. With the exception of the first cervical nerve (C1), all of the spinal nerves are associated with specific dermatomes. Dermatomes are consecutive (do not overlap) in the neck and torso regions. In the arms and legs, adjacent dermatome innervations overlap. The apparently uneven dermatome arrangement in the arms and legs is due to the uneven rate of nerve growth into the limb bud at the embryonic stage.

POSTNATAL BRAIN DEVELOPMENT

After birth, the brain does not grow uniformly but rather tends to increase its mass during irregular periods commonly called growth spurts. In an analysis of brain-body weight ratios, it was found that consistent spurts in brain growth occur from 3 months to 1.5 years of age and also from ages 2 to 4, 6 to 8,

Environmental Influences on Brain Size

The simplest measure of the effects of environment on the nervous system is brain size. Environmental influences on animal brain size have been investigated, and it has been found that exposure to an enriched environment increases brain size. Domestic animals have certain cerebral cortical areas that are as much as 10% to 20% smaller than those of animals of the same species raised in the wild. Increases in the density of glia cells, the number of dendritic spines, and the size of synapses also result from exposure to an enriched environment. These changes are more pronounced if enriched experience is given early in life. In addition to having these anatomical changes, enriched animals can perform better than their impoverished counterparts on a number of learning and memory tests.

10 to 12, and 14 to 16 years of age. The increment during the first spurt was about 30% by weight, and increments during subsequent growth spurts were about 5% to 10% by weight. Paradoxically, the increases take place concurrently with losses of neurons, dendrites, and synapses, and are probably due to an increase in the growth of the cell processes that remain. As the brain continues to grow, the ability to think, learn, and remember grows in parallel. Significantly, the first four brain-growth stages coincide with the ages of onset of the four main stages of intellectual development.

■ **Learn more about development of the nervous system** Search the Internet for *neural tube*, *cell migration*, *myelination*, and *dermatome*.

3 Facts About Our Senses

Our senses are extensions of the nervous system that allow us to perceive our internal and external environments. These senses have been described as "windows for the brain" because it is through them that awareness of the environment is possible. A stimulus must be received before the sensation can be interpreted and necessary body responses coordinated. The senses permit us to experience pleasure and allow us to hear sounds, see dangers, taste foods, smell flowers and other scents, feel shapes and textures, and perceive pain.

TOUCH AND PAIN

Touch and pain are called somatic senses because the receptors that enable us to use these senses are located in the skin (Figure 3.1). For touch, the skin contains a myriad of receptors that convert mechanical energy (from touch) into nerve impulses, which are transported by the peripheral nerves to the spinal cord. The information then travels in the dorsal part of the spinal cord to specialized nuclei in the brain stem. From the brain stem, the information travels to the thalamus and then to the cerebral cortex where the touch stimuli that triggered the original impulse are interpreted as touch. One type of tactile receptor is called the **Meissner's corpuscle,** which is numerous in the hairless portions of the body such as the eyelids, lips, tip of the tongue, fingertips,

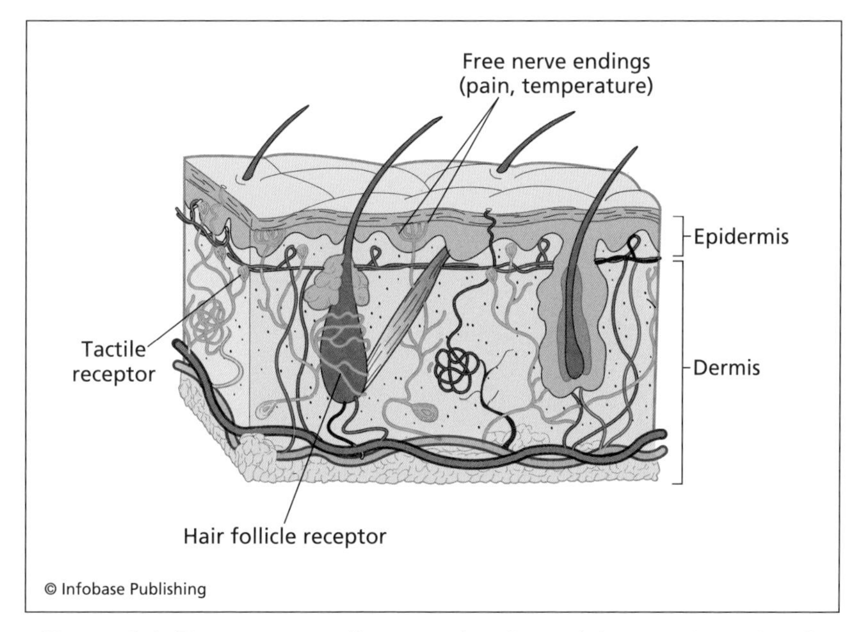

Figure 3.1 Free nerve endings send pain and temperature signals through the spinal cord and on to the brain. Touch (tactile) receptors, such as Pacinian corpuscles, are located in both the inner (dermis) and outer (epidermis) layers of the skin.

palms of the hands, and soles of the feet. These receptors allow for the sensations of light touch and they also function when a person touches an object to determine its texture. Another type of touch receptor is the **Pacinian corpuscle.** This specialized receptor responds to pressure changes and vibratory stimuli. Pacinian corpuscles produce action potentials when the skin is rapidly indented.

The skin has special receptors to detect changes in temperature called thermoreceptors. There are two types of thermoreceptors: cold and warm. Cold receptors are excited by decreases in skin temperature, while warm receptors respond to increases in temperature.

For humans, pain is an unpleasant sensory experience that evokes a multitude of autonomic (blood pressure and heart rate increases) and emotional reactions. These facts suggest that the system that detects painful stimuli is connected to every other response system in our nervous system and underscores the importance of the pain system for the preservation of life. The principal receptors for pain are the **free nerve endings.** Several

Phantom Pain

Phantom pain is frequently experienced by a person who has lost a limb. After loss of the limb, the severed sensory neurons heal and function in the remaining portion of the appendage. Impulses in these severed neurons are interpreted in the brain as arising from their normal source, the amputated region, and they are often painful. This pain is strange because it is perceived as arising from an appendage that no longer exists. Many people with phantom limbs say the pain is unbearable. Scientists have studied people with phantom limbs to determine the cause of this mysterious pain and concluded that the trouble starts in a part of the brain known as the sensory cortex. The sensory cortex carries a rough map of the body, called a homunculus or "little man"—each body part in the homunculus is wired to its corresponding portion of the real anatomy. When a body part is lost, the corresponding part of the brain is not able to handle the loss and rewires its circuitry to make up for the lost signals from the missing part. The rewiring might occur in one of two ways. Nerve impulses in the sensory cortex might begin to course down previously untraveled pathways. Or neighboring neurons in the cortex may invade the territory left empty because sensations are no longer being received. This rewiring may be responsible for the abnormal sensations, including pain.

million free nerve endings are distributed throughout the skin and internal tissues. Pain receptors are sparse in certain **visceral** organs and absent within the nervous tissue of the brain. Although free nerve endings are specialized to respond to tissue damage, some receptors that respond to mechanical stimulation can respond to painful stimulation if they are sensitized (for example, by inflammation).

The protective value of pain receptors is obvious. The perception of pain has survival value because it alerts the body to an injury, disease, or organ dysfunction. Complete absence of pain can be a handicap. Some rare individuals are born without the capability to feel pain. They characteristically have many injuries that heal poorly or remain unhealed and susceptible to infection. They may fracture bones without ever realizing it, have mutilated fingers and toes, or incur serious burns. The condition takes several different forms. Some patients have a selective loss of pain receptors; others have apparently normal receptors, so in these cases the disorder is probably within the central nervous system. This type of disorder results from a defect in neural crest differentiation and the system responsible for pain and temperature sensation is lost. Neurons that detect pain derive from the neural crest, and they can only survive if they are stimulated by nerve growth factor (NGF). Mutations in the gene that encodes the receptor for NGF correlate with the defective development of these neurons. People with congenital insensitivity to pain go through life in danger of destroying their bodies because they do not realize the harm they are doing.

SMELL AND TASTE

The sense of smell in humans is not as highly developed compared to other vertebrates. We do not have to rely on smell for communicating or for finding food. Smell and taste are closely related senses in that they both use receptors that detect chemical stimuli. Smell receptors cells are located in the lining of the nasal cavity. The sensory pathway for the smell sense consists of several neural segments. The nerve fibers coming out from the nasal receptors unite to form the olfactory nerves, which travel through the skull and terminate in the olfactory bulbs. The olfactory tract arises from the olfactory bulb and into the olfactory portion of the cerebral cortex, where chemical signals are interpreted as odors and cause the perception of smell. Thousands of distinct odors can be distinguished by people who are trained in this capacity (as in the perfume industry).

The sense of taste uses receptors clustered together into taste buds, which respond to chemical stimuli and transmit these signals by cranial nerves to the cerebral cortex for interpretation. The taste buds are specialized sensory organs that are found on the tongue and soft palate. There are five basic modalities of taste, known as **gustation:** sweet, sour, bitter, salty, and **umami.** Because taste and smell use chemoreceptors, they complement each other. We often confuse a substance's smell with its taste; and if we have a head cold or hold our nose while eating, food seems to lose its flavor.

HEARING

The ear contains receptors that convert sound waves into nerve impulses (Figure 3.2). Sound waves funnel into the outer ear. They pass along a narrow tube, the ear canal, to a small patch of rubbery skin at its end, the eardrum, and make it vibrate. The eardrum is connected to a row of three tiny bones linked together, the malleus (hammer), incus (anvil), and stapes (stirrup). The vibrations pass along these bones. The stapes presses against a fluid-filled, snail-shaped part called the cochlea, deep inside the ear. The vibrations pass as ripples into the fluid inside the cochlea. Here, they shake thousands of tiny hairs that stick

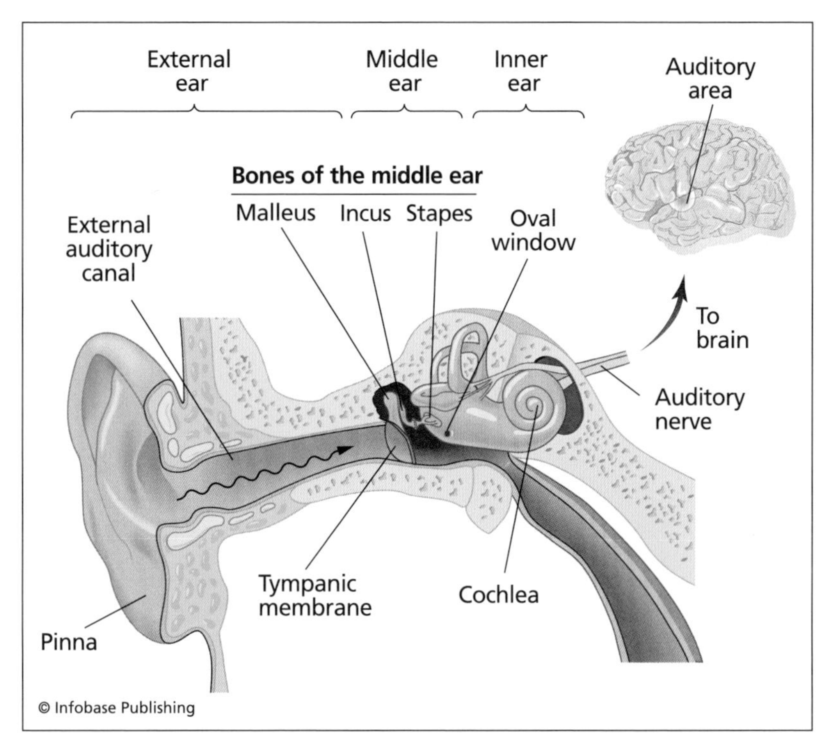

Figure 3.2 The ear converts sound into nerve impulses that are transmitted to the auditory area of the brain.

into the fluid from hair cells. As the hairs shake, the hair cells make nerve signals, which travel along the auditory nerve to the temporal lobe of the brain.

VISION

The eyes are organs that refract (bend) and focus the incoming light waves onto sensitive photoreceptors (receptors that are activated by light) on the retina at the back of each eye (Figure 3.3). Nerve impulses from the stimulated photoreceptors are conveyed through the optic nerves, which converge at the **optic chiasm.** The optic tract is a continuation of optic nerve fibers that enter the brain. The optic tracts continue traveling through the brain to the thalamus and then to the occipital lobe of the cerebral cortex, where the nerve impulses are interpreted as vision. In order for visual information to have meaning, it must be associated with past experience and integrated with information from other senses. Some of this higher processing takes place in areas within the temporal lobes. Experimental removal of these areas from monkeys impairs their ability to remember visual tasks that they previously learned and hinders their ability to associate visual images with the significance of the object.

Numerous disorders and diseases afflict the eyes. One of the most common is a cataract, a clouding of the lens in the eye that leads to a gradual blurring of vision and the eventual loss of sight. A cataract is not a growth within or upon the

Vertigo

The ear contains receptors that respond to movements of the head. Maintaining equilibrium is a complex process that depends on constant input from the vestibular (balance) organ located in both ears. Visual input from the eyes, tactile receptors from the skin, and receptors from the muscle tendons and joints also provide sensory input that is vital for maintaining equilibrium. Vertigo is the sensation of spinning or whirling that occurs as a result of a disturbance in equilibrium due to a disorder in the vestibular system. Vertigo is one of the most common health problems in adults. At least 40% of people in the United States experience vertigo at least once during their lifetime. Prevalence is slightly higher in women and increases with age. Severe vertigo can be disabling and may result in complications such as irritability, loss of self-esteem, depression, and injuries from falls.

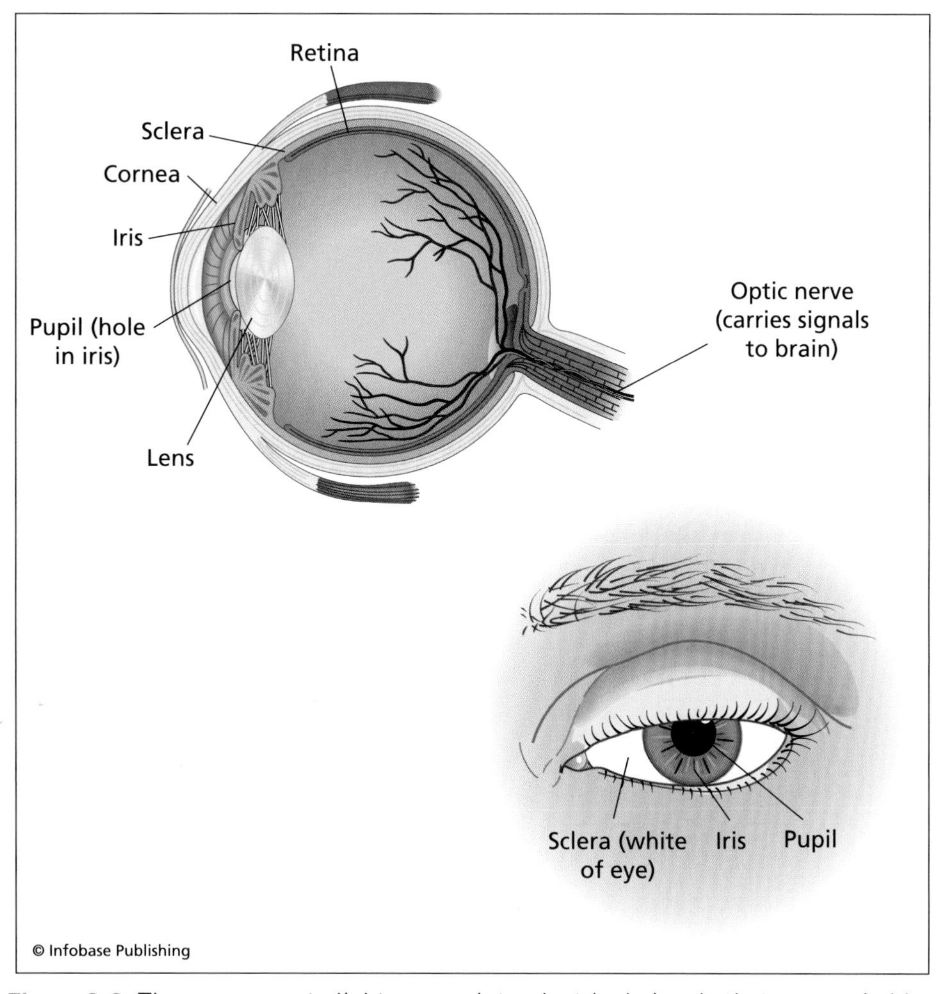

Figure 3.3 The eye converts light energy into electrical signals that are carried by the optic nerve to the brain. This illustration shows a cross section of the eye *(top)* and the exterior of the sensory organ *(bottom)*.

eye but a chemical change in the protein of the lens caused by injury, poisons, infections, or age degeneration. Cataracts are the leading cause of blindness. A cataract can be removed surgically; special contact lenses or thick lenses for glasses are other treatment options.

There are two distinct professional specialties concerned with the structure and function of the eye. Optometry is the paramedical profession concerned with assessing vision and treating visual problems. Ophthalmology is the specialty of medicine concerned with diagnosing and treating eye diseases. Although the eyeball is an extremely complex organ, it is quite accessible to examination. Various techniques and instruments are used during an eye examination. A cycloplegic drug is instilled in the eyes to dilate (enlarge) the pupils. A Snellen chart is used to determine the visual acuity of a person standing 20 feet from the chart; a reading of 20/20 is considered normal for the test. The meaning of the fraction 20/20 is that the first number represents the distance the person is standing from the chart (20 feet). The second number represents the distance from which the average eye can see the letters on a certain line of the eye chart.

■ **Learn more about the senses** Search the Internet for *pain receptor*, *umami*, *cochlea*, and *photoreceptor*.

4 Facts About Our Movements

Each of us has fewer than one million motor neurons with which to control the muscles in the body. Without them, we would be unable to communicate with the outside world, be it by our movements or our speech. Our nervous system makes us capable of an enormous range of complex movements, from automatic unconscious movements, such as postural adjustments, to completely voluntary ones, such as playing a sport.

THE MUSCLE-NERVE INTERFACE

The motor neurons in the spinal cord send their axons to the different muscles in our body. The axons make contact with the muscle fibers at the microscopic level. The area where nerve fibers interact with muscle fibers is called the neuromuscular junction, which is really a synapse between a nerve and a muscle. Nerve impulses traveling down the motor neurons cause the muscle fibers at which they terminate to contract. The terminals of motor neuron axons contain the neurotransmitter **acetylcholine.** The simplest example of the muscle-nerve interface is the reflex arc. A reflex arc implies an automatic, unconscious, protective response to a situation that allows the body to maintain a stable internal environment. The five components of the reflex arc are the receptor, sensory neuron, integrating center (which could be the spinal cord or the brain stem), motor neuron, and effector. An electrical impulse is initiated at the receptor (for example, tapping the knee). This impulse travels to the spinal cord (the integrating center) through the sensory neuron. The sensory neuron synapses on the motor neuron. The motor neuron then sends an impulse to the effector organs, muscles of the thigh, where they contract to produce a jerking reaction (the knee-jerk reflex).

One common type of reflex is the flexor reflex, which is initiated when a person encounters a painful stimulus and needs

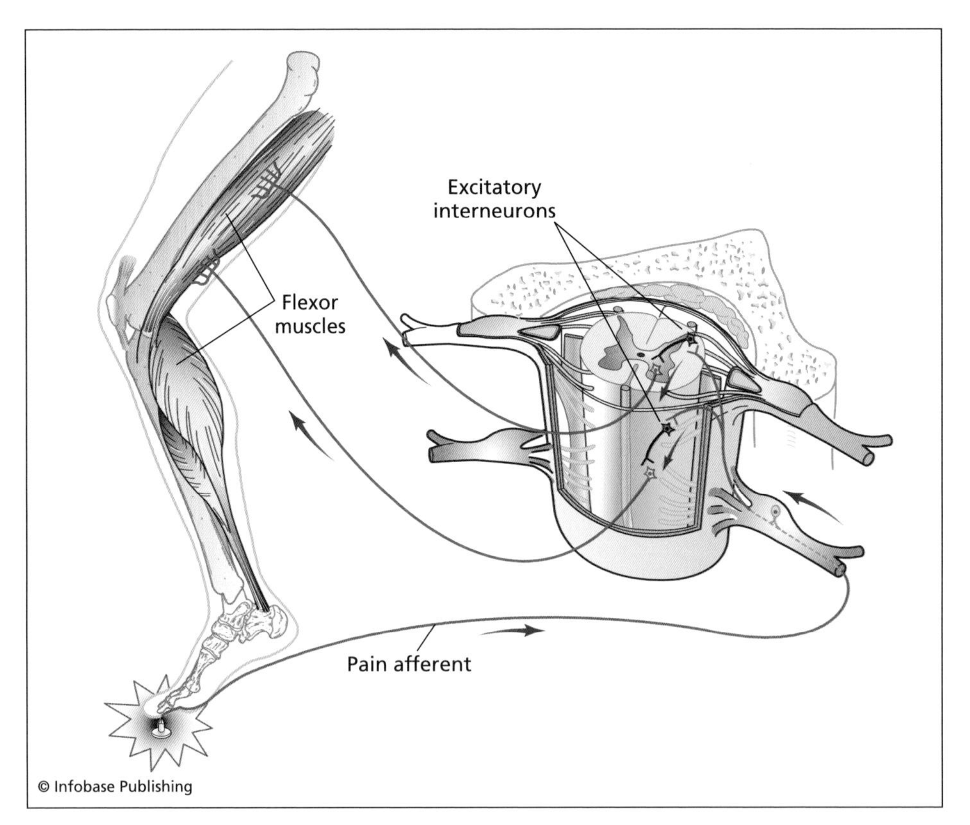

Figure 4.1 The flexor reflex occurs after pain receptors in the skin are stimulated (such as after stepping on a tack, as illustrated above). Sensory neurons then transmit the pain signal to the spinal cord via an afferent nerve. The signal is then relayed to the muscles, which contract to withdraw the injured limb from the source of pain.

to withdraw a limb (Figure 4.1). As the receptor in the skin is stimulated, sensory neurons transmit the impulse to the spinal cord, where other neurons are activated. Then, impulses are directed through motor neurons to flexor muscles that contract in response. Simultaneously, opposing muscles are relaxed so that the injured limb can be quickly withdrawn from the harmful source of stimulation.

From the information above, it is obvious that a great deal of motor control happens at the spinal cord level. Neuronal circuits in the spinal cord organize the order and timing of the motor activity underlying locomotion. This process is called a "central pattern generator." This central pattern generator has been demonstrated in experiments with cats. The cerebral cortex in these animals is removed experimentally, but they are still able

Curare

For thousands of years, native people in the jungles of South America have used extremely potent poison arrows. The poison used in these arrows is called curare, which is a dried extract obtained from the vine *Strychnos toxifera*. Death from curare is caused by asphyxia, because the respiratory muscles become relaxed and then paralyzed. The principal chemicals of curare are alkaloids that affect transmission between nerve and muscle. Specifically, the alkaloid interferes with the activity of the neurotransmitter acetylcholine, blocking the neuromuscular junction. The horror of curare poisoning is that the victim is very much awake and aware of what is happening until the loss of consciousness. Consequently, the victim can feel the progressive paralysis but cannot do anything to call out or gesture. If artificial respiration is performed throughout the ordeal, the victim will recover and have no ill effects.

to walk on a treadmill. This is because the action of locomotion is embedded as a pattern that does not require modulation from the brain. In humans, there is a great deal more control from upper brain structures such as the cerebellum, the basal ganglia, and the cerebral cortex.

THE CEREBELLUM

The cerebellum is the second largest structure in the brain (the largest is the cerebrum). It is located in the posterior aspect of the cranial cavity (Figure 4.2). The cerebellum has a thin, outer layer of gray matter, called the cerebellar cortex, and a thick, deeper layer of white matter. There are also three bundles of nerve fibers, called cerebellar peduncles. These structures support the cerebellum and provide it with tracts for communicating with the rest of the brain.

The principal function of the cerebellum is to coordinate muscle contractions by recruiting precise motor units within the muscles. Impulses for voluntary muscular movement originate in the cerebral cortex (outer layer of the cerebrum) and are coordinated by the cerebellum. The cerebellum constantly initiates impulses to selective motor units for maintaining posture and muscle tone. The cerebellum also adjusts to incoming impulses from receptors within the muscles, tendons, and joints. The cerebellum is also involved in equilibrium because damage to the cerebellum can cause general disequilibrium and vertigo.

It is not surprising to find that the cerebellum has connections with many parts of the brain because it is involved in so many functions. The cerebellum is connected with the spinal cord to help maintain posture and muscle tone. Connections with the cerebral cortex help to coordinate voluntary movements. Finally, connections with the vestibular organs coordinate maintenance of equilibrium and motor learning. The hallmark of cerebellar

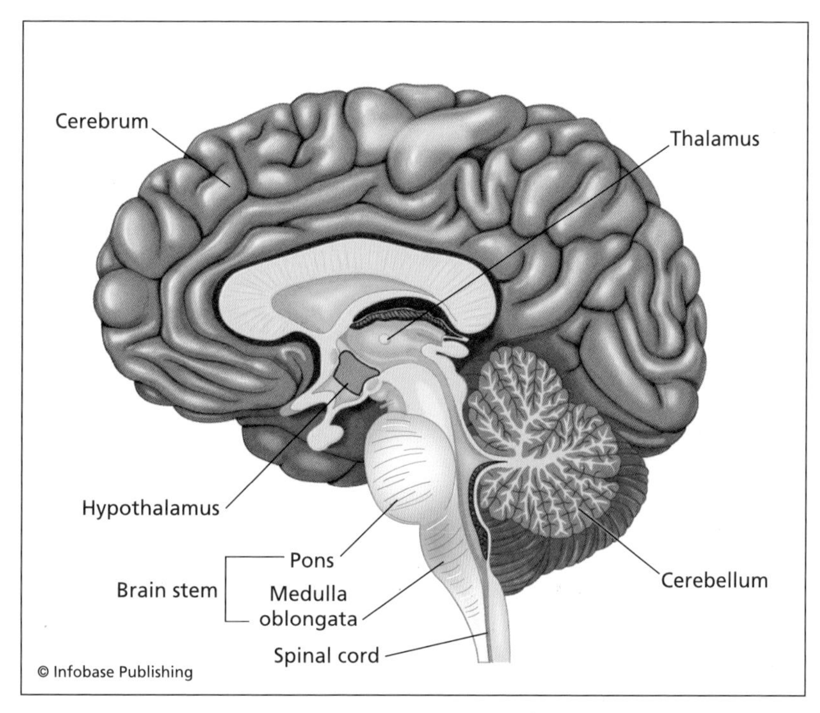

Figure 4.2 The cerebellum helps control movement and balance. It is located beneath the cerebrum and directly behind the pons, which is the upper portion of the brain stem.

disease is a lack of coordination in the absence of weakness or sensory loss. Many symptoms of cerebellar dysfunction are displayed as incorrect timing in the activation of muscles.

THE BASAL GANGLIA

The basal ganglia are specialized masses of gray matter located deep within the white matter of the cerebrum (Figure 4.3). The main nuclei of the basal ganglia are the **caudate nucleus, putamen, globus pallidus, substantia nigra,** and the **subthalamic nucleus.** The relationships between the nuclei of the basal ganglia are by no means completely understood. The caudate nucleus and

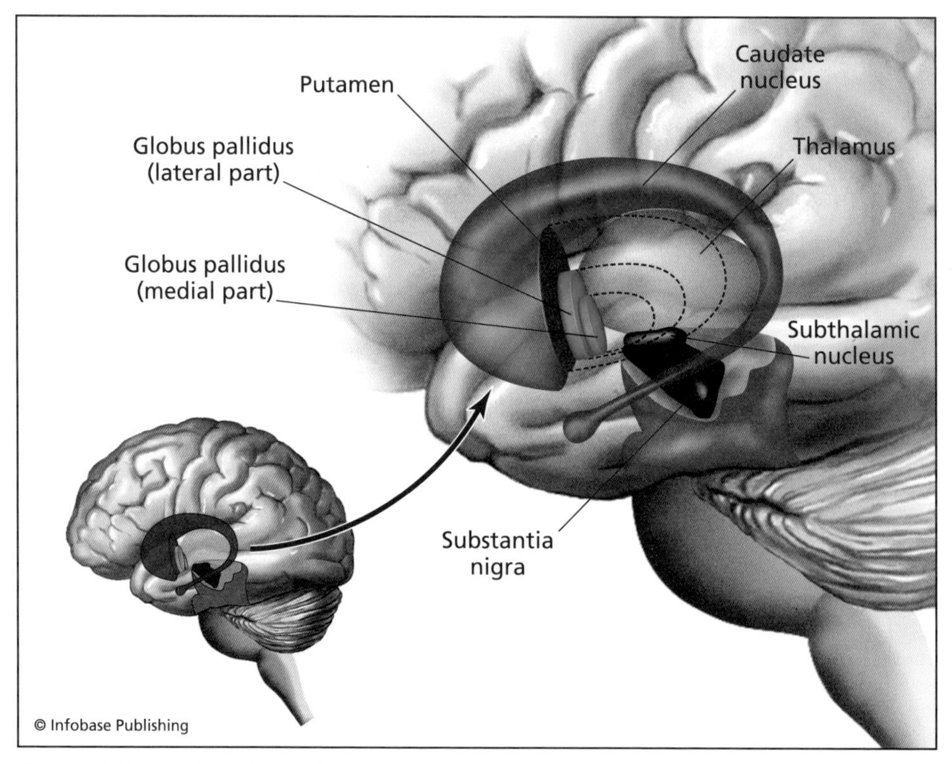

Figure 4.3 The basal ganglia consist of five separate structures that are clustered around the thalamus.

putamen receive most of the input from the cerebral cortex; in this sense, they are the doorway into the basal ganglia. The substantia nigra receives input from the caudate nucleus and the putamen, and sends information right back. The globus pallidus also receives input from the caudate nucleus and the putamen, and is in communication with the subthalamic nucleus.

The function of the basal ganglia is often described in terms of a "brake hypothesis." To sit still, you must put the brakes on all movements except those reflexes that maintain an upright posture. To move, you must apply a brake to some postural reflexes, and release the brake on voluntary movement. The basal ganglia are this "brake." The caudate nucleus and putamen control unconscious contractions of certain muscles, such as those of the upper extremities involved in involuntary arm movements during walking. The globus pallidus regulates muscle tone necessary for specific, intentional body movements.

Dysfunctions in specific nuclei of the basal ganglia result in specific deficits. Huntington's disease or chorea is a hereditary disease of unwanted movements. It results from degeneration of the caudate nucleus and putamen, and produces continuous dance-like movements of the face and limbs. A related disorder is hemiballismus, entailing flailing movements of one arm and leg, which is caused by damage to the subthalamic nucleus. The most common disorder of the basal ganglia is Parkinson's disease.

CEREBRAL CORTEX CONTROL OF MOVEMENTS

The cerebral cortex is the ultimate controller of voluntary movement. Control is effected by direct and/or indirect projections from the cortex to all the subsystems mentioned before (motor neurons in the spinal cord, cerebellum, and basal ganglia). The motor areas of the cerebral cortex consist of the primary motor cortex and the premotor areas. It is in the primary motor area where we find large neurons called Betz cells that send their long axons all the way down to the spinal cord to contact motor neurons and exert control for fine movements (such as hand control). This pathway is called the **corticospinal tract**, and it is well developed in primates, including humans.

The motor and premotor areas in the cortex receive inputs from all the other systems that exert control over movements, including the cerebellum and the basal ganglia. Motor information is integrated in the motor areas of the cortex, and constant feedback is transmitted back and forth between these areas. Sensory areas are also involved in motor integration, since it is

Parkinson's Disease

Parkinson's disease is the most common and probably the best-known disease involving the basal ganglia. This disease affects approximately 1.5 million Americans. Between 50,000 and 60,000 new patients are diagnosed each year. The symptoms are variable in relative severity and onset, but they usually include tremor, rigidity, and slowness in movement. The tremor is called a "resting tremor" because it happens even when a person is sitting still. This tremor is characterized by a constant movement of the hands, which increases during emotional stress. The rigidity is caused by increased tone in all muscles. Finally, people with Parkinson's disease have decreased blinking, an expressionless face, and the absence of the arm movements normally associated with walking. Parkinson's disease is caused by the progressive loss of neurons that produce a neurotransmitter called dopamine in the substantia nigra.

necessary to gather information from the senses to respond with appropriate motor programs. The premotor areas of the cortex are predominantly concerned with the planning of movements.

Lesions of the primary motor areas of the cortex may cause weakness, predominantly in the distal muscles of the contralateral side of the body (for example, if there is a lesion on the left motor cortex, there will be deficits on the right side of the body. Lesions of the premotor areas impair the ability to execute purposeful movement. Lesions of the descending corticospinal tract result in hyperactive reflexes and weakness because the descending control that keeps reflexes in check is damaged.

■ **Learn more about the neuroscience behind movement** Search the Internet for *basal ganglia*, *motor neuron*, *Parkinson's disease*, and *motor cortex*.

5 Facts About Brain Control of Body Functions

At any given time, the body is performing many tasks to maintain **homeostasis.** The nervous system is the ultimate controller of these functions that are performed autonomously and without our awareness. The part of the nervous system in charge of these functions is the autonomic nervous system (ANS). The ANS helps regulate the activities of cardiac muscle (heart), smooth muscle (gut), and glands (endocrine system). The ANS has three major divisions: sympathetic, parasympathetic, and enteric.

THE SYMPATHETIC SYSTEM

The neurons of the sympathetic division are located in the spinal cord from where they send their axons toward the different organs in the abdominal and thoracic (chest) cavities. The sympathetic nervous system activates the body to "fight or flight," largely through the release of epinephrine (adrenaline) from the adrenal glands. Mass activation of the sympathetic division prepares the body for intense physical activity in emergencies: The heart rate increases, blood glucose rises, and blood is diverted to the muscles and away from the visceral organs and the skin. Some of these effects are listed in the table on the next page.

Table 5.1 Sympathetic and Parasympathetic Actions

EFFECTOR	SYMPATHETIC ACTION	PARASYMPATHETIC ACTION
Heart	Increases rate and strength of contraction	Decreases rate; no direct effect on the strength of contraction
Bronchial tubes	Dilates	Constricts
Iris of eye	Dilates pupil	Constricts pupil
Sex organs	Constricts blood vessels, ejaculation	Dilates blood vessels, erection
Blood vessels	Generally constricts	No innervation for many
Sweat glands	Stimulates	No innervation
Intestine	Inhibits motility	Stimulates motility and secretion
Liver	Stimulates conversion of glycogen to glucose	No effect
Adipose tissue	Stimulates free fatty acid release from fat cells for energy requirements	No effect
Adrenal medulla	Stimulates secretion of epinephrine and norepinephrine	No effect
Salivary glands	Stimulates thick, viscous secretion	Stimulates profuse, watery secretion

THE PARASYMPATHETIC SYSTEM

The neurons of the parasympathetic division are located in the midbrain and hindbrain and in the sacral portion of the spinal cord. Many of the parasympathetic neurons send their fibers through the long vagus nerve that travels through the diaphragm to the abdominal cavity. As the vagus nerve travels through the body cavity, it gives off branches to innervate different organs, such as the heart, lungs, esophagus, stomach, pancreas, liver, small intestine, and the upper half of the large intestine. The neurons in the sacral spinal cord innervate the lower half of the large intestine, rectum, and urinary and reproductive organs.

The effect of the parasympathetic system is in many ways opposite to the effect of the sympathetic system. The parasympathetic system is most active in ordinary, restful situations. After a stressful episode, it decreases the heart rate and blood pressure and stimulates the digestive system to process food. The parasympathetic system is dominant during relaxation or calm, quiet activities.

The sympathetic and parasympathetic systems work together to orchestrate the numerous complex activities continuously taking place in the body (Figure 5.1). These two systems accomplish this by releasing chemicals into the different effector organs. Most organs have dual innervations from both systems.

CHEMICALS USED BY THE AUTONOMIC NERVOUS SYSTEM

The autonomic nervous system uses epinephrine (from the adrenal glands), norepinephrine, and acetylcholine as neurotransmitters to perform its functions. Release of norepinephrine and epinephrine has both excitatory and inhibitory effects. The diverse effects of epinephrine and norepinephrine can be understood in terms of the "fight or flight" response to stress. Their actions produce an increase in cardiac pumping, **vasoconstriction**, and thus reduced blood flow to the visceral organs, as well as dilation of the pulmonary bronchioles.

The effect of acetylcholine on effector organs is always excitatory. Acetylcholine acts on receptors found on the surface of

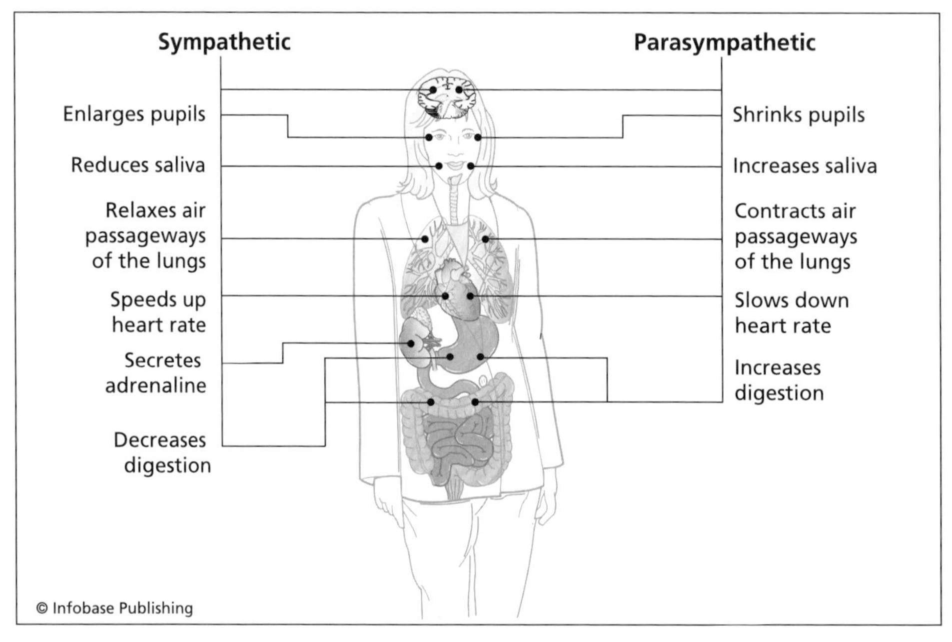

Figure 5.1 The actions of the parasympathetic and sympathetic nervous systems are often opposite of each other. For example, while the sympathetic nervous system is responsible for speeding up the heart rate, the parasympathetic system acts to slow down the heart rate.

cells. One type of receptor, called muscarinic receptors, produces slowing of the heart, dilation of the pupils, and increased gastrointestinal activity (for digestive purposes). The other type of receptor is called the nicotinic receptor. The drug nicotine, derived from the tobacco plant, specifically stimulates this receptor. This is also the main receptor at the neuromuscular junction where the effector organ (muscle) is activated and movement ensues.

THE ENTERIC NERVOUS SYSTEM

The enteric nervous system controls the function of the gastrointestinal tract, pancreas, and gallbladder. It contains local sensory neurons as well as motor neurons, and is responsive to alterations in the tension of gut walls and changes in the chemical environment of the gut. The enteric motor neurons control the muscle of the gut, local blood vessels, and secretion of the mucosa lining the gut walls. The human enteric nervous system has about one billion neurons, approximately as many as the entire spinal cord. All of these neurons are embedded in the wall of the gastrointestinal tract (gut, pancreas, and gallbladder).

The enteric nervous system is relatively independent of the central nervous system (CNS). Disruption of enteric connections to the CNS results in little or no impairment in the function of the gastrointestinal tract. Congenital and acquired derangements in the structure or function of the enteric nervous system are well recognized as causes of digestive tract disease. Examples of such diseases include small intestinal motility disorders, gastric outlet obstructions, and megacolon.

Autonomic Dysreflexia

Autonomic dysreflexia is a serious condition that produces rapid elevation in blood pressure, which can lead to stroke. It occurs in 85% of people with spinal cord injuries. Lesions of the spinal cord first produce the symptoms of spinal shock, characterized by a loss of reflexes. After a period of time, reflexes return in an exaggerated state, due to the absence of descending inhibitory influences, and the visceral organs become hypersensitive. Patients in this state have difficulty emptying their urinary bladders, exaggerated goose bumps, cold skin, and profuse sweating.

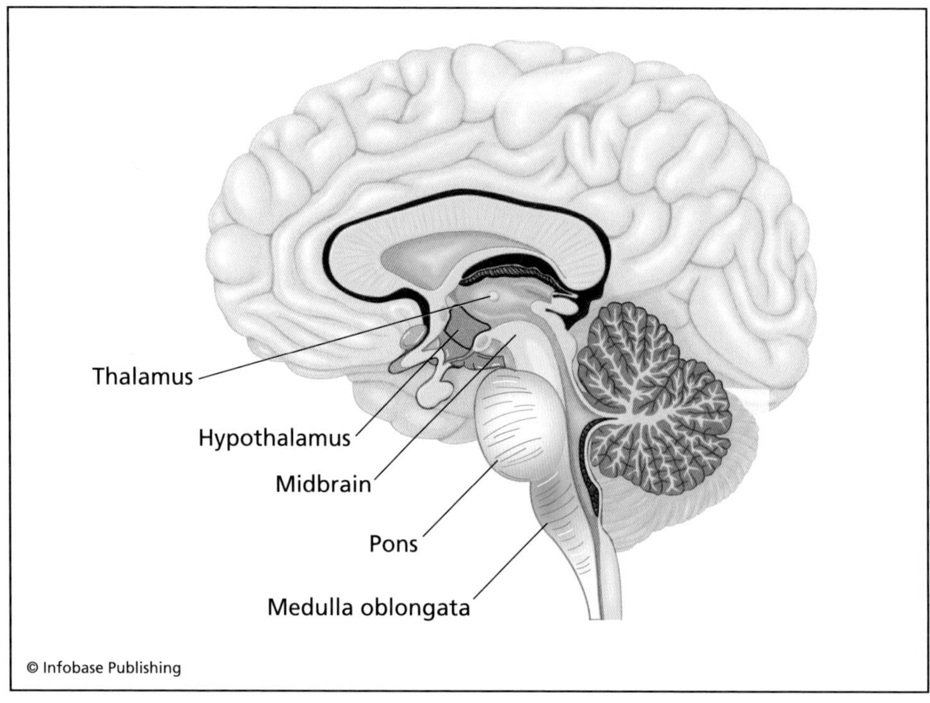

Figure 5.2 The medulla oblongata in the brain stem is largely responsible for regulating involuntary functions such as breathing, swallowing, and heartbeat. It also communicates with higher centers in the brain, such as the hypothalamus.

CONTROL OF THE AUTONOMIC NERVOUS SYSTEM BY HIGHER BRAIN CENTERS

Visceral functions are regulated, to a large degree, by both the sympathetic and parasympathetic systems. Nonetheless, a great deal of information from the viscera reaches brain centers that modify the activity of the neurons of the autonomic system. The medulla oblongata in the brain stem is the area that most directly controls the activity of the ANS (Figure 5.2). In this region, we find areas for the control of the cardiovascular, pulmonary (lung), urinary, reproductive, and digestive systems. Much of the sensory input to these centers travels in the sensory fibers of the vagus nerve.

Although the medulla oblongata regulates the activity of autonomic neurons directly, the medulla is itself responsive to regulation by higher brain areas. One of these areas is the **hypothalamus**, the brain region responsible for the control of body temperature, hunger, thirst, regulation of hormones, and, together with the cerebral cortex, various emotional states.

Another higher brain area involved in modulation of the ANS is the **limbic system**, a group of fiber tracts and nuclei that forms a ring around the brain stem. It is involved in basic emotional drives, such as anger, fear, sexual interest, and hunger. The involvement of the limbic system with the control of autonomic function is responsible for the visceral responses that are characteristic of these emotional states. Blushing, pallor, fainting, breaking out in a cold sweat, a racing heartbeat, and "butterflies in the stomach" are some of the visceral reactions that, as a result of autonomic activation, accompany emotions.

Hypothermia

Hypothermia is defined as a core body temperature of less than 35°C (95°F). It may range from mild (32°–35°C [90°–95°F]) to profound (less than 30°C [86°F]). Several types of hypothermia exist. Induced hypothermia protects organs in cardiac and transplantation surgery and preserves isolated tissues such as blood and skin. Profound cold (cryotherapy) is used to destroy tissues and preserve cells such as sperm. Accidental hypothermia occurs if heat loss exceeds heat production or maintenance. Incidental hypothermia develops in neurologic, metabolic, and dermatologic diseases that interfere with body temperature control, including hypothyroidism, diabetes, stroke, and a brain tumor affecting the hypothalamus.

EXERCISE AND THE AUTONOMIC NERVOUS SYSTEM

The autonomic nervous system plays a key role in the regulation of the cardiovascular response during exercise. At the onset of exercise, the central nervous system generates a cardiorespiratory pattern appropriate to the pattern of the exercise. The cardiorespiratory pattern then initiates a slowing down of parasympathetic activity to the heart and an increase in ventilation rate, and is also probably involved in the resetting of the arterial **baroreflex** toward higher blood pressures.

At the onset of exercise, it is generally accepted that heart rate is increased primarily by the sympathetic system. As exercise continues or its level increases, further elevations in heart rate may occur. Additionally, there is increased sympathetic outflow to the peripheral circulation and sweat glands to keep the body at appropriate temperatures. Receptors located in muscles provide important signals relative to the activity and blood flow of exercising muscles. In general, we assume that mechanical activation of the muscle receptor signals muscle activity and that the resulting activity contributes to the regulation of sympathetic outflow. Activation of chemical receptors by substances released in the muscle as a result of exercise also contributes to the regulation of peripheral blood circulation and cardiac output.

■ **Learn more about brain control of body functions** Search the Internet for *autonomic nervous system*, *limbic system*, and *fight or flight.*

6 Facts About Sleep

We spend about 8 hours per day, 56 hours per week, 240 hours per month, and 2,920 hours per year sleeping, close to one-third of our lives. What is sleep and why do we do it? According to a simple behavioral definition, sleep is a reversible behavioral state of perceptual disengagement from and unresponsiveness to the environment. Sleep, in an evolutionary sense, is an old behavior; depending on the definition of sleep used, even insects exhibit sleep. Most living organisms display rhythmic changes in the state of their organs and in their behavior. Our body has an internal pacemaker process called a biological clock. The most common biological clock runs on a 24-hour period (such as a sleep-wake cycle, also know as a circadian rhythm), but it is adjusted and modified by the external environment. Sleep is a complex array of physiological and behavioral processes.

THE RETICULAR ACTIVATING SYSTEM

The reticular activating system (RAS) is a complex neural pathway within the brain stem and the thalamus. It receives messages from neurons in the spinal cord and from many parts of the nervous system, and communicates with the cerebral cortex. The RAS is responsible for maintaining consciousness (wakefulness) and for arousal from deep sleep.

When the RAS is very active and sending many messages into the cerebral cortex, a state of mental and physical alertness is noted. When RAS activity slows, however, sleepiness results. If the RAS is severely damaged, a deep, permanent coma may result.

THE PROCESS OF SLEEP

Sleep is a state of unconsciousness during which there is altered electrical activity in the cerebral cortex and from which a person can be aroused by external stimuli. When signals from the RAS slow down so that the cerebral cortex is deprived of activating input, a person may lapse into sleep. For this reason, we find it easy to go to sleep, even when we are not particularly tired, if there is nothing interesting to occupy the mind. But although we tend to be wakeful in the presence of attention-holding stimuli, there is a limit beyond which sleep is inevitable.

Consciousness and Coma

One definition of consciousness is a behavioral state in which an individual is awake and exhibits some degree of alertness. Levels of alertness can vary and may include behavioral states in which an individual is fully alert, alert but confused, lethargic, nonresponsive to certain types of sensory stimulation, or stuporous. Coma is defined as a loss of consciousness that continues for an extended period of time and is not sleep related. Unlike sleep, coma is characterized by a significant decrease in the level of brain activity. Coma may be reversible or irreversible. Loss of consciousness may occur due to metabolic disturbances (for example, diabetes or alcohol consumption), strokes, or traumatic head injuries.

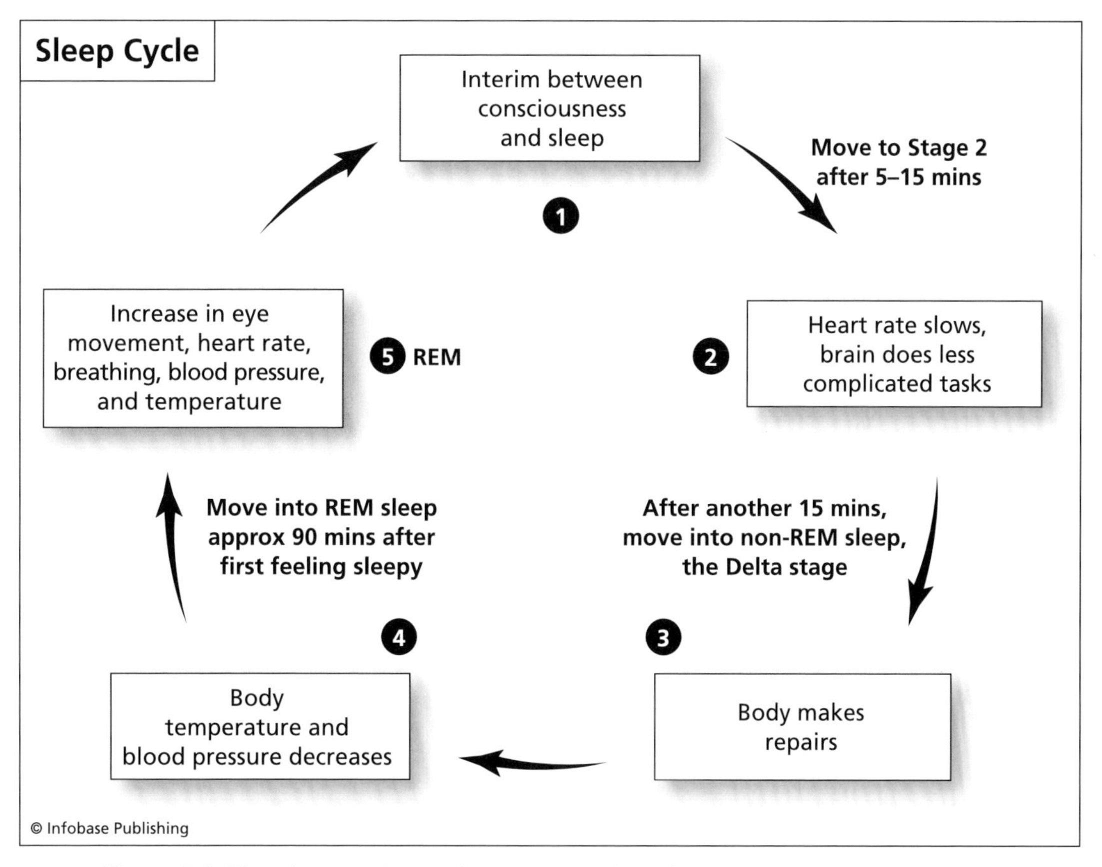

Figure 6.1 The sleep cycle consists of stages in which certain physiological changes occur. For example, during REM sleep, there is an increase in eye movement, heart rate, and breathing compared to the previous stage.

Two main stages of sleep are recognized, non-REM sleep and REM sleep (Figure 6.1). REM is an acronym for "rapid eye movements." During non-REM sleep, sometimes called slow wave sleep, the metabolic rate decreases, breathing slows, and blood pressure decreases. Every 90 minutes or so, a sleeping person enters the REM stage of sleep for a time. During this stage, which accounts for about one-fourth of total sleep time, the eyes move rapidly about beneath the closed but fluttering lids.

Sleep researchers have shown that everyone dreams, especially during REM sleep. Dreams may result from the release of norepinephrine within the RAS, which generates stimulating impulses that are fed into the cerebral cortex. However, not everyone remembers his or her dreams the next morning.

Why sleep is necessary is not completely understood. Apparently, only higher vertebrates with fairly well-developed cerebral cortices have complex sleep patterns divided into different stages. When a person stays awake for unusually long periods, fatigue and irritability result, and even routine tasks cannot be performed well. It is thought that perhaps certain waste products accumulate within the nervous system, and sleep gives the nervous system an opportunity to dispose of them.

Not only is non-REM sleep required, but REM sleep is apparently also essential. In sleep deprivation experiments performed with human volunteers, lack of REM sleep makes subjects anxious and irritable. After such experiments, when subjects are permitted to sleep normally again, they go through a period when they spend more time than usual in the REM stage. After recovery, there is no apparent long-lasting damage.

Many types of drugs alter sleep patterns and affect the amount of REM sleep. For example, sleeping pills may increase the total sleeping time but decrease the time spent in REM sleep. When a person stops taking such a drug, several weeks may be required before normal sleep patterns are reestablished.

AGE AND SLEEP

The percentage of REM sleep is highest during infancy and early childhood, drops off during adolescence and young adulthood, and decreases further in older age. Of course, infants require the greatest amount of sleep. As parents know, total sleep time typically becomes shorter during childhood and may become

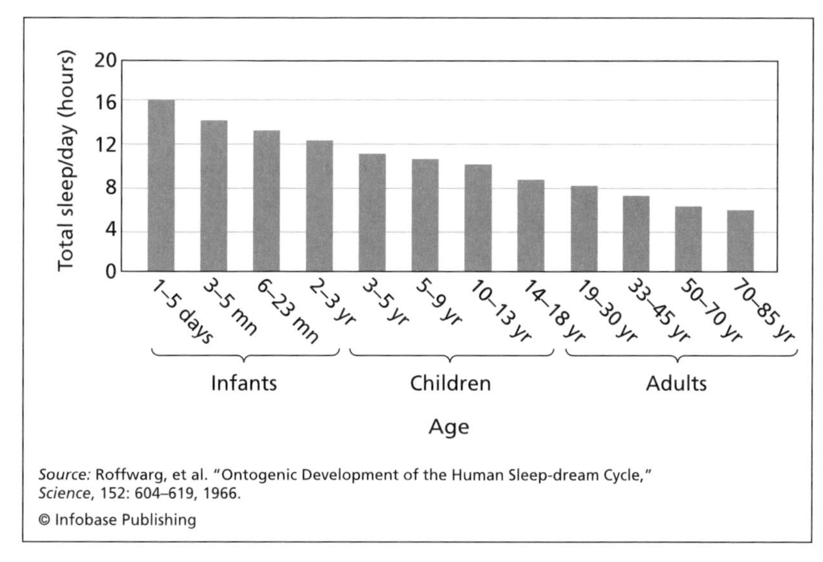

Figure 6.2 The total amount of sleep required by different age-groups is illustrated in the chart above.

longer again in adolescence. The time dimensions of sleep change again as one ages: Older people get less total sleep than younger people do, and older people commonly enter REM sleep quicker and stay there longer (Figure 6.2).

SLEEP DISORDERS

Sometimes, disturbances in sleeping patterns are the result of a medical disorder with no direct connection to the process of sleep. In these cases, the disturbance in sleep is a symptom of the underlying disease. Nonetheless, there are specific disorders linked to the process of sleep.

Insomnia

Insomnia is the chronic inability to obtain the necessary amount or quality of sleep to maintain adequate daytime alertness.

Insomnia is a symptom that can be caused by a variety of physiological and psychological disorders. It is most common in older people, women, and lower socioeconomic groups.

The most common cause of insomnia is psychological problems, such as depression and anxiety (marital, family, and job-related stressors). Other causes include physiological sleep disorders, disturbance of normal circadian rhythm (from night-shift work or jet lag, for example), and as a natural consequence of aging. A variety of medical problems such as central nervous system trauma, infections, degenerative conditions, thyroid dysfunction, uremia, and alcoholism also produce sleep disturbances. In addition, certain drugs, either when administered or withdrawn, may result in sleep disturbances.

There is no effective long-term medication for insomnia. Although hypnotic drugs help for short periods, they may actually aggravate insomnia after several days.

Sleep Apnea

People with sleep apnea have normal respiratory function when they are awake but stop breathing for short periods when asleep. Apnea may last 10–180 seconds and may repeat several hundred times a night. Patients are awakened by apnea, but it may not be recognized. Sleep apnea syndrome occurs 6 to 15 times more frequently in males than in females. Almost all people with sleep apnea are heavy snorers, and most are overweight. Due to the disturbance of sleep, people with sleep apnea suffer from impairment of daily activity. They may develop psychiatric disorders, such as depression, and cardiovascular disorders, such as hypertension.

Narcolepsy

Narcolepsy is characterized by irresistible sleep attacks, lasting 5–30 minutes, during the day. The frequency of attacks varies among people and may change during the course of a person's life. Attacks of narcolepsy may occur several times to 200 times each day. An attack is more likely to occur when the person is involved in passive and boring work, but narcolepsy can be triggered by strong emotions as well. Narcolepsy is typically accompanied by one or more of the following symptoms: cataplexy (sudden loss of muscular tonus, causing the person to fall down while fully conscious), sleep paralysis (an inability to move that develops in the transition between arousal and sleep), and hypnagogic hallucinations (vivid visual and auditory sensations occurring at the onset of sleep).

People who suffer from narcolepsy go into the REM sleep stage directly from an awake state. However, they have a lower proportion of REM sleep than do other people. Narcolepsy tends to run in families. It usually begins at puberty and continues for the remainder of the person's life.

THE FUNCTION OF SLEEP AND DREAMS

It is likely that sleep is functionally important because it has persisted throughout the evolution of mammals and birds. In the laboratory, rats that have been deprived of sleep for two to three weeks will die. There are several theories regarding the function of sleep.

- **Conservation of metabolic energy**: The idea that sleep conserves energy is supported by the fact that humans increase their food intake during sleep deprivation. The idea that sleep enforces body rest is supported by the fact that small mammals tend to sleep the most. Since we feel refreshed after sleep, this theory is appealing.
- **Thermoregulation**: There are strong indications that sleep has thermoregulatory functions. Body and brain temperatures are usually reduced during sleep.
- **Neural maturation and mental health**: The idea that REM sleep aids neural maturation is strongly supported by the

association of REM sleep and immaturity at birth across species. Some reports indicate that REM sleep facilitates learning and memory.

What is the function of dreaming? According to Sigmund Freud, the founder of psychoanalysis, dreams are disguised manifestations of strong, unacceptable, unconscious wishes. Much of the impetus for modern dream research was motivated by the interest in the analysis and interpretation of dream content. There are no special procedures for uncovering hidden meanings of dreams. It is not really true that external stimuli of certain kinds can influence the type of dreams you have during the night. For example, restricting fluid intake during a 24-hour period does not lead to the appearance of thirst themes in dreams. Viewing violent or pornographic films does not produce violent or sexual dreams afterward. Most dreams experienced over the course of a night are quite ordinary. There are exceptions, where external stimuli, such as noises or tactile stimulation, can become incorporated into dreams. Dreams

Nightmares and Night Terrors

Nightmares are intense, frightening dreams that lead to waking. They are more common than night terrors. Night terrors are attempts to fight or flee, accompanied by panic and sometimes bloodcurdling screams. Nightmares occur during dream sleep, but night terrors occur during stage 4 sleep. Night terrors are usually brief (one to two minutes), and the person usually cannot remember the episode. Both kinds of events are more common in children than in adults, perhaps because adults are more experienced with disturbing dreams and so are not easily awakened. Both types of events can be sufficiently disturbing to disrupt sleep and lead to insomnia.

have an undeserved reputation of being bizarre because our spontaneous recall of dreams is usually limited to the longer, more exciting dreams that typically occur before morning awakening. In general, a person's mood, anxiety, and expressiveness in dreams are positively correlated with these traits in their waking experience.

Except for some decrease in the clarity of background detail and color saturation, visual dream imagery resembles waking visual imagery. Like waking imagery, most dreams are in color. Perhaps the greatest difference between dreaming and ordinary wakefulness is that we are able to differentiate between real and imagined images only when we are awake. Except for the relatively rare lucid dreams in which we know we are dreaming, all dream images seem real.

■ **Learn more about the brain and sleep** Search the Internet for *circadian rhythm*, *rapid eye movement*, *sleep disorder*, and *dream analysis*.

7 Facts About Language

Language is the remarkable system that allows people to communicate an unlimited combination of ideas using a highly structured stream of sounds. Language is the most accessible function of the brain/mind, and for millennia it has been a central concern of scholars in many disciplines. One definition of language is that it is the ability to encode ideas into signals for communication to someone else.

All human cultures have language, and everywhere people use it creatively to convey new ideas. The design of language is based on two components, words and grammar. A word is an arbitrary association between a sound and a meaning. For example, English speakers use the word *cat* (as opposed to chat, dog, or blicket) to refer to a certain animal, not because the word has any natural connection with this animal but simply because it is a shared convention used by a community of speakers who have all, at some time in their lives, memorized the connection between that word and its meaning. By the age of six years, children comprehend about 13,000 words, and high school graduates have mastered at least 60,000. This means that children connect a new sound and meaning about every 90 waking minutes. The connection is bidirectional—children merely have to hear a word to use it themselves; they do not need molding or feedback.

Grammar is the system that specifies how vocabulary units can be combined into words, phrases, and sentences. It allows us to distinguish, for example, between "man bites dog" and "dog bites man," using the position of the words to convey different meanings. Because grammar is based on a set of rules regarding the combination of words, the number of sentences a speaker can produce grows exponentially with the length of the sentence; there are on the order of 10^{20} grammatically meaningful sentences of 20 words or fewer. Indeed, the number of combinations is infinite.

THE DEVELOPMENT OF LANGUAGE

According to Charles Darwin, founder of the theory of evolution, "Man has an instinctive tendency to speak, as we see in the babble of our young children; while no child has an instinctive tendency to brew, bake, or write." In the first year of life, children work on sounds. They begin to make language-like sounds at five to seven months, babble in well-formed syllables at seven to eight months, and gibber in sentence-like streams by the first year. In their first few months, they can discriminate speech sounds, including ones that are not used in their parent's language. A child's first words are spoken around the time of his or her first birthday, and the rate of word learning increases suddenly around the age of 18 months, which is also the age at which children first string words into combinations. Children at the age of two years begin to speak in rich phrase structures and master the grammatical vocabulary of their language. By the age of three years, children use words grammatically correct most of the time and in general become fluent and expressive conversational partners.

LANGUAGE IN OTHER SPECIES

One might think that if language evolved by a gradual, Darwinian natural selection process, it must have a precursor in

Figure 7.1 A scientist teaches a chimpanzee to communicate using sign language.

lower animals. Nonetheless, communication between animals is dramatically different than that in humans. Animal language is based in three designs: a limited number of calls (to warn for predators or claim territory, for example), a continuous signal that registers some environmental cue (such as distance of a food source), or sequences of randomly ordered responses that serve as variations on a theme (as in birdsong).

Some animals can be trained to mimic certain aspects of human language in artificial settings. In several famous and controversial demonstrations, chimpanzees and gorillas have been taught to use some hand signs based on American Sign Language, manipulate colored switches or tokens, and carry out some simple spoken commands (Figure 7.1). Parrots and dolphins have also learned to recognize or produce ordered sequences of sounds. Such studies have revealed much regarding the cognitive abilities of nonhuman species, but the relevance of these animal behaviors to human language remains questionable. Chimpanzees require extensive teaching to acquire rudimentary abilities, mostly limited to a small number of signs strung together in repetitive sequences, used with the intent to request food. The core design of human language—the formation of words, phrases, and sentences—does not emerge in these animals.

APHASIAS AND LANGUAGE AREAS OF THE BRAIN

Knowledge of the brain regions involved in language has been

The Origins of Sign Language

The specific origins of language are obscure. *Homo habilis*, a species related to modern humans that lived about 2.5 million years ago, left behind stone tools. This indicates that early man may have communicated the skills and movements necessary to make these tools using a primitive language. *Homo erectus*, an early ancestor that spread from Africa across much of Europe from 1.5 million to 500,000 years ago, controlled fire and used a kind of stone hand-axe. Likely, some form of language contributed to such successes.

The first *Homo sapiens*, thought to have appeared about 200,000 years ago and to have moved out of Africa 100,000 years ago, had skulls similar to ours and much more elegant and complex tools than the previous species. They almost certainly had language, given that their anatomy suggests they were biologically very similar to modern humans and that all modern humans have language. The major human races probably diverged about 50,000 years ago, which puts a late boundary on the emergence of the different languages.

gained primarily by the study of **aphasias,** speech and language disorders caused by damage to specific language areas of the brain. These areas are generally located in the cerebral cortex of the left hemisphere (Figure 7.2) in both right-handed and left-handed people.

- **Broca's aphasia** is characterized by halting, effortful verbal output, poor articulation, reduced phrase length, and relatively preserved comprehension. It is associated with a lesion of Broca's area in the frontal lobe (see Figure 7.2).
- **Wernicke's aphasia** is characterized by fluent speech used in sentences, but containing improper or faulty words and impaired comprehension. It is associated with lesions of Wernicke's area in the temporal lobe (see Figure 7.2). Speech is relatively normal in rate, rhythm, and melody, but empty in content. Reading and writing are severely impaired.
- **Conduction aphasia** is characterized by fluent speech and relatively normal comprehension, but the ability to repeat words or phrases on request is disproportionately impaired. It is associated with a lesion in the left parietal region, which disrupts the fibers connecting Broca's and Wernicke's areas.
- **Global aphasia** refers to a nonfluent aphasia associated with markedly impaired comprehension, defective naming, and repetition disturbance. It is associated with a large lesion that may involve the frontal, temporal, and parietal areas.

There are other language deficits that are more specific in nature, and they are associated with more discrete lesions. For example, destruction of the angular gyrus, an area located at the border between the temporal and parietal lobes, causes **anomic aphasia,** a deficit characterized by the inability to name objects.

By virtue of the study of these deficits, a clear picture has emerged regarding the localization and processing of language in the human brain. Broca's area is in charge of the motor

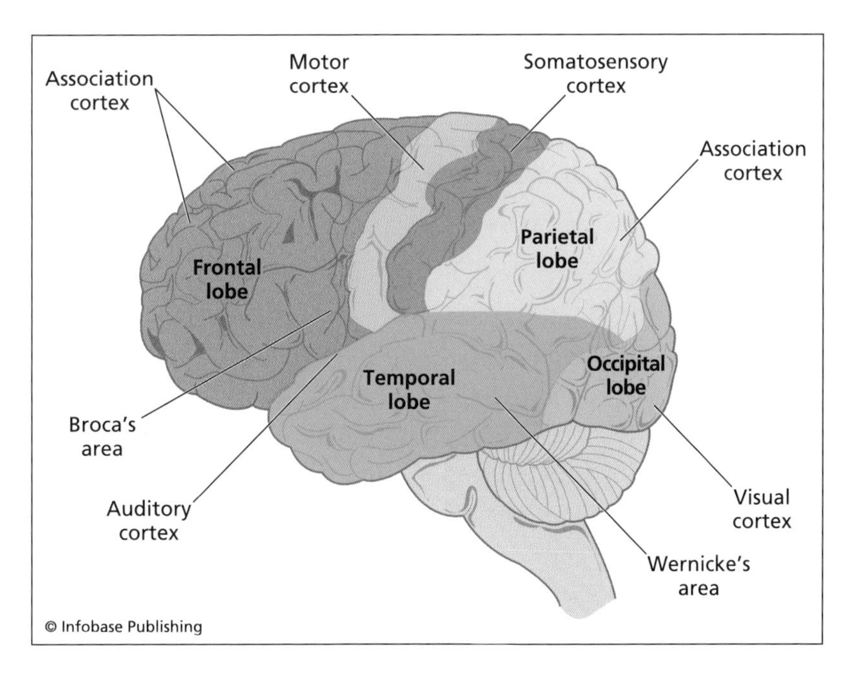

Figure 7.2 Broca's area (located in the frontal lobe) and Wernicke's area (located in the temporal lobe) have been shown to be critical for language acquisition.

aspects of the production of speech. Neural activity in this area causes coordination of the muscles of the pharynx and larynx. At the same time, motor impulses are sent from Broca's area to respiratory muscles to regulate air movement across the vocal cords. The combined muscular stimulation translates thought patterns into speech. This is why lesions of this area affect only the production of speech but not the comprehension of speech.

Wernicke's area is concerned with the comprehension of speech. This area is surrounded by the temporal, parietal, and occipital lobes. Auditory information (temporal lobe), visual information (occipital lobe), and orientation information (parietal lobe) converge on Wernicke's area to provide it with information necessary to understand written and verbal language. Wernicke's area connects to Broca's area to produce responses (verbal or written) to language signals.

OTHER BRAIN AREAS INVOLVED IN LANGUAGE PROCESSING

We have seen that most basic processing of language is found in the left hemisphere. Nonetheless, the right cerebral hemisphere does play a role in language. In particular, it is important for emotional prosody (stress, timing, and intonation of speech). People with right hemisphere lesions may produce inappropriate intonations in their speech and have difficulty interpreting the emotional tone of others. Additionally, people with this type of lesion have difficulty incorporating sentences into a coherent narrative and using appropriate language in particular social settings. They often do not understand jokes. These impairments make it difficult for people with right hemisphere damage to function effectively in social situations, and they are sometimes shunned because of their odd behavior.

When adults with severe neurological disease have the entire left hemisphere removed, they suffer a permanent and catastrophic loss of language. In contrast, when the left hemisphere of an infant is removed, the child learns to speak fluently. Adults do not have this plasticity of function, and this age difference is consistent with other findings that suggest there is a critical period for language development in childhood. Children can acquire several languages perfectly, whereas most adults who take up a new language are saddled with a foreign accent and permanent grammatical errors. When children are deprived of language input because their parents are deaf, they can catch up fully if exposed to language before puberty, but they are strikingly inept if the first exposure comes later.

■ **Learn more about the brain and language** Search the Internet for *aphasia*, *Koko the gorilla*, *Broca's area*, and *Wernicke's area*.

8 Facts About Learning and Memory

For humans, the most important mechanisms by which the environment alters behavior are learning and memory. Learning is the process by which we acquire knowledge about the world, while memory is the process by which that knowledge is encoded, stored, and later retrieved.

Many important behaviors are learned. Indeed, we are who we are largely because of what we learn and what we remember. We learn the motor skills that allow us to master our environment, and we learn languages that enable us to communicate what we have learned, thereby transmitting cultures that can be maintained over generations. But not all learning is beneficial: Learning also produces dysfunctional behaviors, and these behaviors can, in the extreme, constitute psychological disorders.

TYPES OF MEMORY

Clinical studies have suggested that there are two types of memory. **Short-term memory** involves recalling information for only a few moments. When you look up a telephone number in a directory, for example, you generally remember it just long enough to dial it. Should the line be busy and you turn your attention to another task before returning to try again, you would probably have to look up the number again.

Short-term memory depends upon neural circuits that continue to reverberate for several minutes until they fatigue, or until new signals that interfere with the old ones are received.

When a decision is made to store information in **long-term memory**, the brain apparently rehearses the material and then stores it in association with similar memories. Some investigators think that actual changes occur in neurons, which

Amnesia

Amnesia is a partial or complete loss of memory. The causes of amnesia range from psychological trauma to brain damage caused by a head injury, brain tumor, stroke of the blood vessels supplying the brain, or swelling of the brain. There are many types of amnesia. In anterograde amnesia, people have a difficult time remembering new events after suffering damage to the head. They do not tend to forget their childhood or who they are, but they have trouble forming new memories and remembering day-to-day events. In retrograde amnesia, people find it hard to retrieve memories prior to an incident in which they suffered head damage. Sometimes people never remember the seconds leading up to the incident. Korsakoff's syndrome is memory loss caused by alcohol abuse. The person's short-term memory may be normal, but he or she will have severe problems recalling a simple story, lists of unrelated words, faces, and complex patterns.

Traumatic amnesia follows brain damage caused by a severe blow to the head, such as a road accident. It can lead to a loss of consciousness for a few seconds, or to coma. Infantile amnesia refers to the inability of a person to recall events from early childhood. Finally, hysterical amnesia is linked to psychological trauma. It is usually temporary and can be triggered by a traumatic event with which the mind finds it difficult to cope.

then form new connections where the new information is stored. Several minutes are required for a memory to become consolidated in the long-term memory bank. Retrieval of information stored in long-term memory is of considerable interest, especially to students. Some investigators think that once information is deposited in the long-term memory bank, it remains within the brain permanently. When you seem to forget something, the problem may be that you have actually forgotten the search routine that would permit you to retrieve that item for conscious use.

THE CELLULAR BASIS OF LEARNING AND MEMORY

The nerve cells in our brain retain the memory of every thought, every emotion, and every experience. The method neurons use to store these and other memories is by the connections or synapses they make with one another. The modulation of the strength of these synapses makes available a cellular substrate for the process of memory and the storage of learned behaviors.

One of the cellular processes that might be the biological basis for memory is **long-term potentiation** (LTP). LTP is the process by which there is long-lasting strengthening of the connections between neurons. High-frequency stimulations can potentiate the transmission of impulses across synapses for minutes to hours, days, months, or years. This LTP is possible thanks to the intracellular changes that occur after this high-frequency stimulation. Different proteins are activated inside the cell, which contribute to permanent changes inside the nucleus of the cell. These changes alter the way a neuron responds once it is stimulated again.

WHERE IN THE BRAIN ARE MEMORIES STORED?

Clinical studies of amnesia suggest that several different brain regions are involved in memory storage and retrieval. Amnesia has been found to result from damage to the temporal lobe

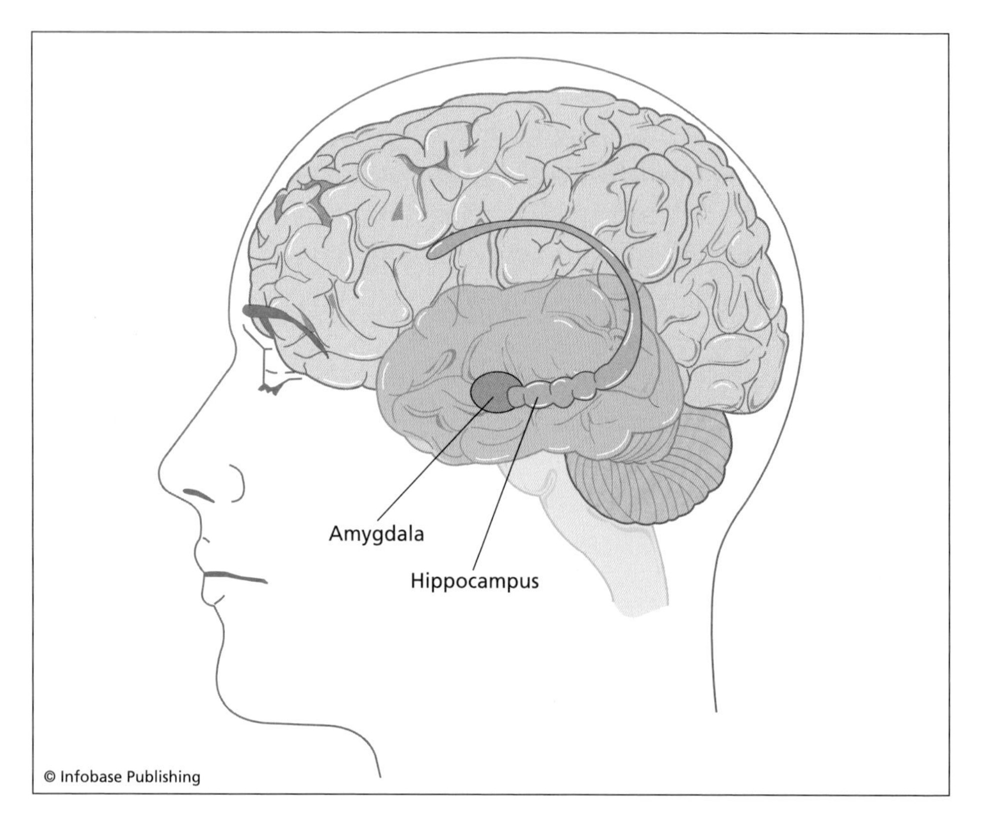

Figure 8.1 The hippocampus is a critical part of the brain for the storage of memories. The amygdala plays a large role in processing emotions.

of the cerebral cortex, hippocampus, and head of the caudate nucleus or the thalamus. The **hippocampus** (Figure 8.1) appears to be required for short-term memory and for the consolidation of that memory into a long-term form. The surgical removal of the left hippocampus due to the presence of tumors impairs the consolidation of short-term verbal memories. Removal of the right hippocampus impairs the consolidation of nonverbal memories. The surgical removal of both left and right hippocampi leaves a patient totally without short-term memory.

Alzheimer's Disease

Alzheimer's disease is an irreversible, progressive disease of the brain that slowly destroys memory and reasoning skills. In the United States, about 4 million people suffer from this disease. About 10% of Americans over the age of 65 and close to 50% of those over 85 years of age suffer from Alzheimer's. It would seem that this disease is an "old age" disease, but there are cases where the onset of Alzheimer's takes place in people in their 40s.

The main sign of Alzheimer's disease is dementia. Dementia is the loss of the normal ability to form new short-term memories, loss of previous long-term memories, and deficits regarding thinking and judgment. Individuals with Alzheimer's also suffer from personality changes, a clue that it is not only cognitive ability that suffers but also higher brain functions. The loss of memories may change these patients' identities, since memories make us who we are, according to many philosophers.

One of the main findings regarding the pathology of Alzheimer's is the rapid loss of neurons in the cerebral cortex, which then appears smaller compared to a normal brain (Figure 8.2). One of the first areas to undergo these degenerative changes is the hippocampus, which explains why memories are the first to suffer. The cause of Alzheimer's disease is unknown at this time, but evidence points to genetic factors being involved, since Alzheimer's tends to run in families.

There is nothing that can be done to slow the loss of neurons. However, there are drugs that people in the early stages of Alzheimer's can take, which are helpful in preventing memory loss, dementia, and other behavioral deficits that come about with this disease.

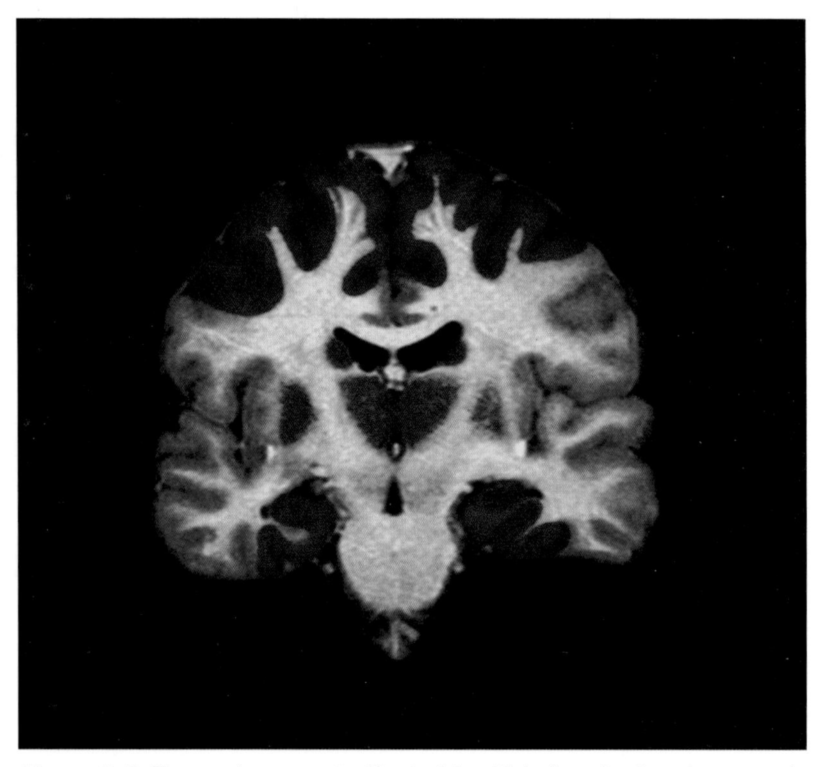

Figure 8.2 The regions most affected by Alzheimer's disease are colored red/purple in this MRI image of the brain.

Factual information is stored in the cerebral cortex, with verbal memories lateralized to the left hemisphere and visuospatial information in the right hemisphere. Electrical stimulation of various regions of the cerebrum of awake patients often evokes visual or auditory memories that are extremely vivid. Electrical stimulation of specific points in the temporal lobe evokes specific memories in such detail that the person will feel that the experience is currently happening. Surgical removal of these regions does not, however, abolish the memory. The amount of memory destroyed by ablation of brain tissue appears to depend more on the amount of brain tissue removed than on the location of the surgery. On the basis of these observations, it appears that memory may be diffusely located in the cerebrum and that stimulation of the correct location of the cerebral cortex then retrieves the memory. There are even examples of olfactory memories being retrieved by stimulation of the part of the cortex concerned with olfactory processing.

EFFECTS OF ENVIRONMENTAL EXPERIENCE ON THE BRAIN

Environmental experience can cause physical as well as chemical changes in brain structure. In one series of studies, a group of rats was provided with an enriched environment, while another group was placed in a deprived environment. Rats in the enriched environment were provided with toys, rat and human interaction, and opportunities to learn. Those in the deprived environment, while given sufficient food, water, and shelter, were deprived of intellectual stimulation and social interaction. After several weeks, rats from each group were killed and their brains were studied. Those exposed to the enriched environment exhibited large cell bodies, greater numbers of glia cells, increased numbers of synaptic contacts, and biochemical changes. Some investigators reported that the cerebral cortex became thicker and heavier. Animals reared in a complex environment may also be able to process and remember information more quickly than those reared in a deprived environment.

Early environmental stimulation can also promote development of motor areas in the brain. For example, rats encouraged to exercise show increased cerebellar development. Such studies linking the development of the brain with environmental experience support the concept that early stimulation is important for the neural, motor, and intellectual development of children.

LEARNING DISABILITIES

There are several types of learning disabilities. The most common and challenging ones are the academic skills disorders,

Figure 8.3 Dyslexia is a disorder that affects one's ability to read and write. In this photo, a girl is being tested for dyslexia by an educational psychologist.

including developmental reading, writing, and arithmetic disorders. Developmental reading disorder, which is also known as **dyslexia**, is quite widespread (Figure 8.3). In fact, reading disabilities affect 2% to 8% of elementary school children. A person can have problems in any of the tasks involved in reading. Investigators have found that a significant number of people with dyslexia share an inability to distinguish or separate the sounds in spoken words. Some children have problems sounding out words, while others have trouble with rhyming games, such as rhyming *cat* with *bat*. Fortunately, remedial reading specialists have developed techniques that can help many children with dyslexia acquire these skills.

A developmental writing disorder may result from problems in the skills areas of vocabulary, hand movement, and memory. For example, a child with writing disability, particularly an expressive language disorder, might be unable to compose complete, grammatical sentences. Finally, children with difficulties recognizing numbers and symbols, memorizing facts, aligning numbers, and understanding concepts like decimals and fractions suffer from a developmental arithmetic disorder, also called dyscalculia. Problems with numbers or basic concepts are likely to show up early. Disabilities that appear in the later grades are more often tied to problems in reasoning.

■ **Learn more about the brain's role in learning and memory** Search the Internet for *amnesia, olfactory memory,* and *dyslexia.*

9 Facts About Emotions and Moods

We are emotional beings. In our brains, we carry the "chemical soup" that makes emotions possible. We know this because chemical imbalances produce disorders of mood and abuse of drugs. In clinical descriptions of emotional states, the term ***mood*** refers to a sustained emotional state of a person, lasting weeks or more. The term ***affect*** refers to an immediate or momentary emotional state (for example, an emotional response like anger or euphoria, which only lasts for a limited amount of time).

Normal affective responses serve important biological functions and range from euphoria, elation, pleasure, and surprise to anger, disappointment, sadness, grief, despair, and even depression. Three of these responses, euphoria, depression, and anxiety, can become so exaggerated that they then become a disease state.

THE NEURAL BASIS OF EMOTIONS

Like perception and action, emotional states and feelings are mediated by distinct neuronal circuits within the brain. In fact, many drugs that affect the mind, ranging from addictive street drugs to therapeutic agents, do so by acting on specific neural circuits concerned with emotional states and feelings. Conscious feeling is mediated by the cerebral cortex, in part by an area called the cingulate cortex, and the frontal lobes. Emotional states are mediated by a family of autonomic, endocrine, and motor responses, which involve structures located underneath the cerebral cortex, including the amygdala, the hypothalamus, and the brain stem. For example, when frightened, we not only feel afraid but also experience increased heart rate and respiration, dryness of the mouth, tense muscles, and sweaty palms, all of which are regulated by these structures.

The peripheral, motor, and autonomic aspects of emotion have preparatory and communicative functions. The preparatory function involves both general arousal, which prepares the body as a whole for action, and specific arousal, which prepares the person for specific behavior. For example, sexual arousal involves an increase of heart rate, a change that prepares the way for physical exertion. In addition, it involves more localized changes, such as **tumescence,** that are specific to sexual behavior. The mechanism of generalized and specific arousal act together to prepare the periphery (muscles, glands, blood vessels) and the cerebral cortex for ongoing or upcoming events.

The **hypothalamus** regulates the motor and autonomic aspects of emotions. It modulates visceral reflexes and coordinates most autonomic reflexes. In this way, the hypothalamus ensures that a well-organized, coherent, and appropriate set of responses is matched to the different emotions. Animals with experimental lesions of the hypothalamus become placid.

THE LIMBIC SYSTEM

The limbic system is a complex set of structures that lies on both sides of and underneath the thalamus, just under the cerebrum (Figure 9.1). It includes the hypothalamus, the hippocampus, the amygdala, the olfactory cortex, the cingulate cortex, the septum, the ventral tegmental area, and the prefrontal cortex. In previous chapters, we discussed the hypothalamus, the hippocampus, and the olfactory cortex. The limbic system is

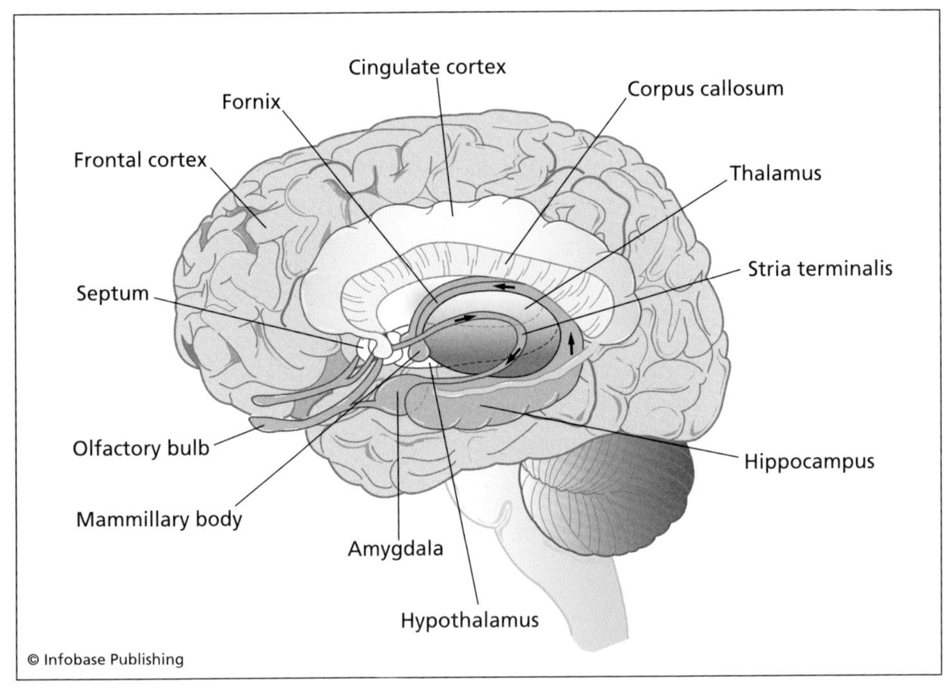

Figure 9.1 The limbic system is a set of brain structures from which feelings and emotions originate.

connected in one direction with widespread cortical areas and in another direction with the hypothalamus.

One classic technique for studying the function of a structure is to remove it or destroy it and then see what happens. When parts of the limbic system are removed, animals suffer from a constellation of deficits called the Kluver-Bucy syndrome, with these characteristics:

- The animals are fearless and placid, showing an absence of emotional reactions. They do not respond to threats, to social gestures by other animals, or to objects they would normally flee from.
- Male animals become hypersexual and are impressively indiscriminate in their choice of sex partners.

- They show an inordinate degree of attention to all sensory stimuli, as though ceaselessly curious. They respond to every object within sight or reach by sniffing it and examining it orally. If the object can in any sense be considered edible, they eat it. Partly because of this, they eat much more than normal animals.
- Although they incessantly examine all objects in sight, they recognize nothing and may pick up the same thing over and over. This is called "psychic blindness."

THE AMYGDALA

Considerable evidence from both humans and experimental animals now indicates that the amygdala intervenes between the regions concerned with the physical expression of emotion (the hypothalamus and brain stem) and the cortical areas concerned with conscious feeling, especially fear (the cingulate, parahippocampal, and prefrontal cortices).

The amygdala is a collection of nuclei in the temporal lobe that receives a great deal of sensory input in a highly processed form. Visceral inputs, particularly olfactory inputs, are especially prominent. Additional visceral information reaches the amygdala indirectly from the hypothalamus, the insular cortex, and the brain stem. Portions of the cingulate cortex also project to the amygdala and are probably responsible for most of the auditory, visual, and other sensory information that reaches this structure.

Fibers leave the amygdala through two major pathways. The first pathway is the stria terminalis, which arches around from the temporal lobe (see Figure 9.1). The second pathway is the ventral amygdalofugal pathway, which spreads as a blanket at the base of the brain. The diffuse spread of the connections from the amygdala gives us a reason to believe that this structure is involved in every emotional state.

As complex as the connections of the amygdala appear, they are dominated by extensive interconnections with the septal area and the hypothalamus, as well as with the prefrontal cortex. This puts the amygdala in a position to influence behavior patterns and the subjective feelings that accompany these activities. In the first of these two roles, the amygdala can be considered a sort of higher order modulating influence in the hypothalamus. Almost any visceral or somatic activity that can be elicited by stimulating the hypothalamus (including such things as feeding or cardiovascular and respiratory changes) can also be elicited by stimulating some point in the amygdala. The responses to amygdala stimulation tend to be more "natural" than those to hypothalamic stimulation, building up gradually and then subsiding slowly.

The role of the amygdala in subjective feelings has also been indicated in electrical stimulation studies in animals. When an animal's amygdala is stimulated, the animal most often stops whatever it was doing and becomes very attentive. This may be followed by responses of defense, raging aggression, or fleeing. Amygdala stimulation in humans can cause a variety of emotions, but the most common is fear accompanied by all its normal manifestations, such as dilation of the pupils, release of adrenaline, and increased heart rate (Figure 9.2). Conversely, destruction of the amygdala causes a great decrease in aggression, and as a result animals are tame and placid. This is part of a different kind of memory deficit, one that impairs the ability to learn or remember the appropriate emotional and autonomic responses to stimuli.

OTHER BRAIN AREAS INVOLVED IN EMOTIONS

Stimulation of the frontal cortex produces autonomic responses (increases in blood pressure, dilation of the pupils, salivation,

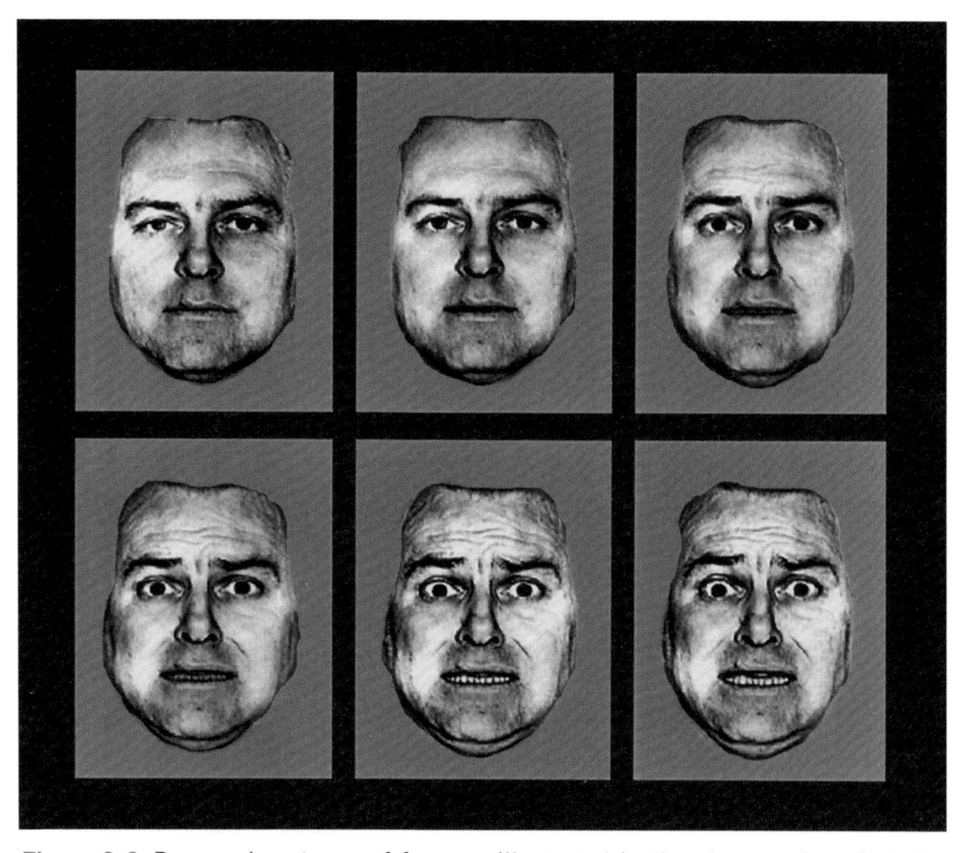

Figure 9.2 Progressive stages of fear are illustrated in the above series of photographs. In the upper left, the man is at ease. At bottom right, he shows the greatest amount of fear. The researchers behind this study found that as the subject expressed increased fear, there was a corresponding increase in activity of the amygdala.

and inhibition of gastrointestinal contractions), suggesting that this area is involved in general arousal. Lesions of the frontal cortex reduce the normal aggressiveness and emotional responses of primates. Animals with these lesions sometimes fail to show anger when they do not receive expected rewards. Lesions that include the anterior cingulate cortex also reduce chronic pain. This is not due to an effect on the processing of pain but rather an effect on the emotional aspect of pain.

People with these types of lesions do not "care" about the pain anymore.

Early theories of the neural control of emotional states attributed to the hippocampus a major role in coordinating the activity

Anxiety Disorders

Just as grief is a normal response to personal loss, anxiety is a normal response to threatening situations. Perceived threats that generate anxiety may be active and direct or indirect. Anxiety is adaptive—it signals potential danger and can contribute to the mastery of a difficult situation. Excessive anxiety, on the other hand, can be harmful, either because it is too intense or because it is inappropriately provoked by events that present no real danger.

The key feature of anxiety disorders is increased fearfulness accompanied by subjective as well as objective manifestations. The subjective manifestations range from a heightened sense of awareness to a deep fear of impending disaster and death. The objective manifestations are a racing heart, avoidance behavior and signs of restlessness, heightened responsiveness, palpitations, tremor, sweating, increased blood pressure, dry mouth, and a desire to run or escape.

Depression and anxiety usually occur together. Anxiety disorders are the most common psychiatric disorders, found in approximately 15–20% of the general population. Anxiety disorders can be subdivided into several types, based on clinical characteristics and response to medication. These major categories include panic disorder, post-traumatic stress disorder, generalized anxiety disorder, social phobia, and obsessive-compulsive disorder.

of the hypothalamus and cerebral cortex. Subsequent experimental studies on both monkeys and humans showed that the coordinating role is carried out by the amygdala. The role of the hippocampus in emotions is more related to memory of emotions and learning different patterns of emotional responses. Indeed, many aspects of our primary emotional responses are learned. With experience, we depend increasingly on cognition to evaluate the significance of our environment, and visceral sensations probably play a less important role. For example, the emotional responses of an infant are based purely on visceral sensations (temperature, hunger, etc.). As maturation progresses, the child relies less on crying to meet his or her needs but can now communicate them.

MOTIVATION

Motivational states involve neural mechanisms that are widely distributed throughout the brain, but the hypothalamus plays a prominent role. The hypothalamus is very much involved in regulating various behaviors that are directed toward **homeostasis.** For example, obtaining food and water and temperature regulation are some of these behaviors. The hypothalamus contributes to these behaviors by receiving information (incentives). The hypothalamus, through its control of hormonal release and the autonomic nervous system, is also involved in the regulation of behavioral states such as stress and anxiety.

Many functions of the hypothalamus can be understood in terms of control systems that respond to specific physiological needs. However, motivated behaviors are also regulated by factors that do not directly correspond to needs. One such important variable is the pleasure principle. The neural systems that mediate reward and pleasure use a variety of chemicals, but the main one used is **dopamine.**

THE PLEASURE PRINCIPLE

Pleasure is, without a doubt, a key factor in controlling the motivated behaviors of humans. We will sometimes even subject ourselves to deprivations to heighten the pleasure obtained when the deprivations are relieved (skipping lunch so as to enjoy dinner more) or to obtain pleasure by satisfying other needs (dieting to look attractive). The neural mechanisms of pleasure

Drug Abuse and the Brain

Addictive drugs such as cocaine, amphetamines, opiates, and nicotine act like positive reinforcers. Animals will readily press a lever to give them an intravenous infusion of amphetamine, for example. Drugs of abuse act on the reward and pleasure circuits of the brain.

The main chemical found in these circuits is dopamine. Psychoactive drugs increase the levels of dopamine in the ventral tegmental area. Cocaine and amphetamines raise the level of dopamine in the nucleus accumbens, while nicotine does so in the pathway between the limbic system and the cerebral cortex. This enhancement of dopamine may serve as a constant reinforcement for cigarette smoking.

Addiction involves more than just the positive reinforcement derived from the drug and the resulting anticipation of the euphoria it produces. Two other features characterize addiction. Tolerance refers to the progressive adaptation to the doses that produce euphoria, so that higher and higher doses are needed to achieve the same effect. Dependence refers to the negative physical reactions of withdrawal from the drug, such as nausea. Thus, drug abuse is not only driven by the rewarding effects of the drug, but also by trying to avoid the bad effects of withdrawal.

are poorly understood, but it seems reasonable to think that they overlap with brain mechanisms concerned with reward. It is this principle that is involved in producing addictions.

■ **Learn more about the brain and emotion** Search the Internet for *amygdala*, *mood disorder*, and *cingulate cortex.*

10 Facts About Higher Brain Functions

I think, therefore I am.

—René Descartes (1596–1690)

We live on a small blue planet that circles an average star, one of hundreds of millions of stars that make up our galaxy. It is amazing to think that in the middle of this vastness, human intelligence emerged. Intelligence, as we know it, arises from trillions of connections between neurons in our brains. It is our thoughts that make up our personalities and define our self-image. Any type of disturbance to the ensemble of neurons can produce profound changes in our personality and the way we think. Our thoughts, and the way we interact with our environment and other human beings, arise from our cerebral cortex.

THE CEREBRAL CORTEX

The cerebral cortex is a sheet of neurons and their connections with one another, about 2.5 square feet in area. This sheet contains approximately 30 billion neurons, connected by 100,000 kilometers of axons and dendrites. The cerebral cortex is characterized by numerous folds and grooves called convolutions, which increase the area of the cerebral cortex. This arrangement has allowed for the continuous increase in size of the human cerebral cortex during the course of

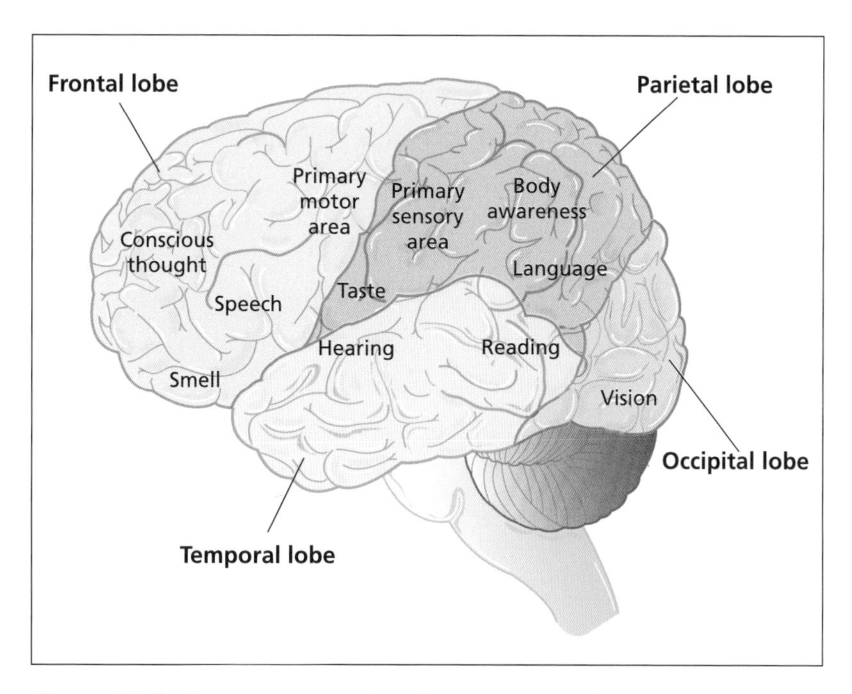

Figure 10.1 The outer part of the brain, known as the cerebral cortex, can be labeled according to its functions, such as taste, speech, and hearing.

evolution. The cerebral cortex has a great deal to do with the abilities and activities at the highest level of development in humans, such as language and abstract thinking.

The cerebral cortex is the seat of many functions that are distributed among several areas (Figure 10.1). The sensory areas of the cortex deal with our vision, hearing, taste, and touch (see Chapter 3). The motor areas deal with the generation and patterns of our movements (see Chapter 4). Language and memory are also generated in specialized areas of the cortex (see Chapters 7 and 8). The present chapter will deal with higher functions originating from the frontal and parietal areas of the cerebral cortex.

CEREBRAL DOMINANCE

Most of the functions of the cerebral cortex apply equally to both hemispheres. However, language function is lateralized in the human brain, and the hemisphere that is more important for the comprehension and production of language is called the dominant hemisphere. Nearly all right-handed people (more than 95%) have dominant left hemispheres. Left-handed people are more likely than right-handers to have dominant right hemispheres, but still the majority of left-handers are left-dominant. Thus, the side that is dominant is correlated to some extent to handedness, but regardless of whether an individual is left-handed or right-handed, the left hemisphere is more likely to be dominant.

Connections of the Cerebral Hemispheres

Information in the cerebral cortex is transported back and forth between the cerebral hemispheres through the corpus callosum, a bundle of fibers interconnecting the hemispheres. It contains more than 300 million axons. Many of the sensory modalities transfer information through this fiber bundle. Severing of the corpus callosum has been used as a treatment of last resort for a few patients suffering from epilepsy, to prevent seizures from spreading from one hemisphere to the other. This type of surgery has given rise to "split-brain" patients, who, because their brain hemispheres are unable to communicate with each other, show a number of unusual symptoms. For example, if a split-brain patient is shown a familiar image in his or her left visual field (and thus processed in the right hemisphere of the brain), the patient will not be able to say what the image is. This is because the information received by the right hemisphere cannot cross over to the left side, where language is processed.

In addition to the cases of "split brain," there are other "disconnecting" syndromes that follow cerebral damage in humans. One classic example is the syndrome called pure word blindness.

People with this rare condition are able to write but are unable to read anything, even words they have just finished writing. This syndrome arises because the language areas in the parietal cortex are cut off from the visual areas in the occipital cortex. Therefore, visual information cannot be passed to the language areas, and the person is not able to read; but since the connection of the language areas to the motor areas is still intact, the person is able to write or verbalize language.

THE PARIETAL CORTEX AND SPATIAL ORIENTATION

The parietal cortex is mainly concerned with integration of sensory and motor information to form **cognition** and to construct a spatial coordinate system to represent the world around us. Individuals with lesions in the parietal lobe show striking deficits, such as abnormalities in body images and spatial relations. Two of the most common syndromes arising from parietal lobe damage are agnosia and apraxia. Agnosia (from the Greek word for "lack of knowledge") is the inability to recognize objects. A person may not be able to recognize an object by visualizing it, but he should be able to recognize it by touch or hearing. Apraxia (from the Greek word for "lack of action") is an inability to perform an action, even though the muscles required are perfectly sound and able to perform. An apraxic person might be unable to touch her nose with her index finger when asked to imitate the examiner's movements, but would be capable of doing it on her own if her nose itched.

PERSONALITY AND THE FRONTAL CORTEX

The frontal lobes are considered our emotional control center and home to our personality. This part of the brain expanded dramatically during mammalian evolution. The first clue that the frontal cortex was involved in personality traits came in the nineteenth century from the unfortunate accident affecting Mr. Phineas Gage (see sidebar). The frontal lobes are extremely vulnerable to injury due to their location at the front of the cranium. Patients with frontal lobe damage have few spontaneous facial expressions. One of the most common effects of frontal lobe damage is dramatic changes in social behavior. A person's personality can undergo significant changes after an injury to the frontal lobes. Sexual behavior can also be affected by frontal lesions, causing abnormal sexual behavior as well as reduced sexual interest.

Various means of separating the frontal cortex from the rest of the brain (procedures called frontal lobotomies) were used in the first half of the twentieth century as treatment for certain severe **psychoses.** Individuals treated this way became carefree and often apparently euphoric, which was the beneficial effect

Phineas Gage

In 1848, Phineas T. Gage, the foreman of a railroad construction crew, was setting a charge of explosives with a 13-pound (5.9kg), 3.5-foot (1.1m) iron tamping rod. The charge exploded and blew the tamping iron through the front of his head, destroying a good deal of his frontal cortex (Figure 10.2). It is said that despite his appalling injury, he did not lose consciousness for very long and appeared curiously indifferent to his situation. However, his personality changed remarkably. Before the accident, he was hardworking, responsible, clever, and respectable. After the accident, he seemed to have lost most of his awareness of social responsibilities. He wandered aimlessly from job to job, exhibiting himself and his tamping iron in various carnivals, and was tactless and impulsive in his behavior, not concerned about his future or the consequence of his actions. "Gage was no longer Gage" was said by his friends and doctors. He died 13 years later after, developing epilepsy.

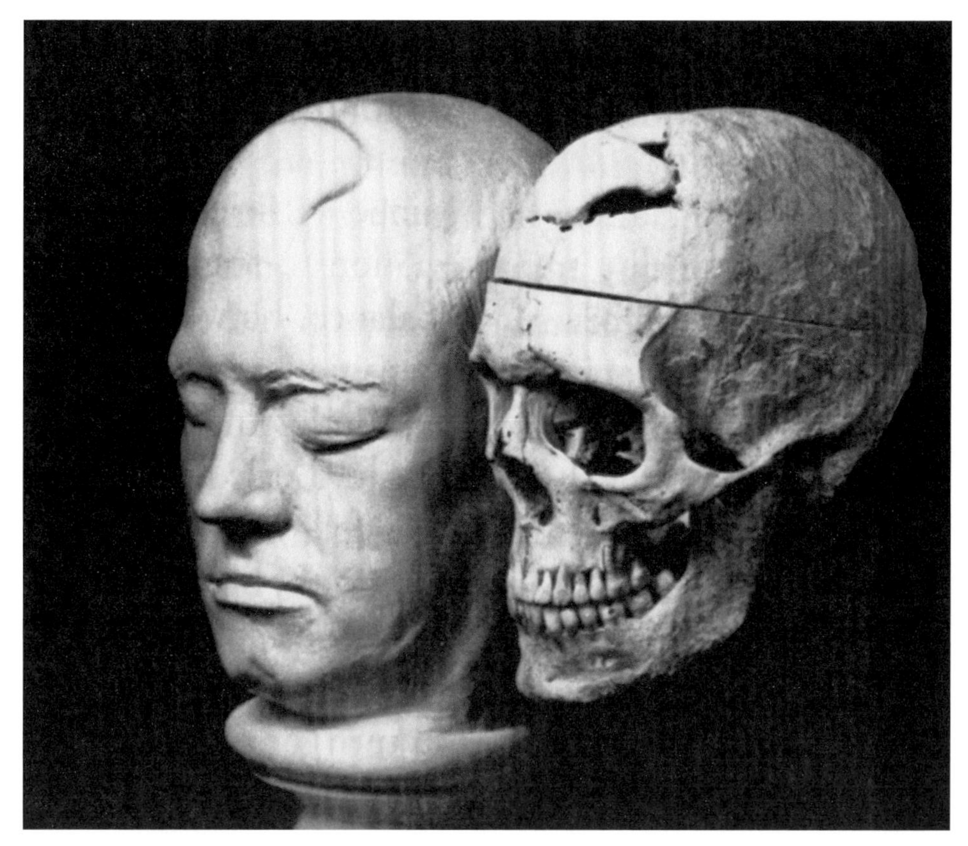

Figure 10.2 A death mask of Phineas Gage is seen beside his skull, which had been fractured by an iron tamping rod.

sought. Someone suffering from intractable pain, for example, would admit that there was no decrease in the pain after frontal lobotomy but would no longer be bothered by it. Unfortunately, many also were inclined not to observe social norms in their behavior, and powers of concentration, attention span, initiative, and spontaneity all suffered.

DISORDERS OF THOUGHT: SCHIZOPHRENIA

Consider the following case history: When Mrs. T was 16 years old, she began to experience her first symptom of schizophrenia—

profound feelings that people were staring at her. These bouts of self-consciousness soon forced her to end her public piano performances. Her self-consciousness led to withdrawal, then to fearful delusions that others were speaking of her, and finally to suspicions that they were plotting to harm her. At first, Mrs. T's illness was intermittent, and the return of her intelligence, warmth, and ambition between episodes allowed her to complete several years of college, to marry, and to rear three children. She had to enter a hospital for the first time at the age of 28 when she began to hallucinate. Now, at 45, Mrs. T has seen dinosaurs on the street and live animals in her refrigerator. While hallucinating, she speaks and writes in an incoherent way. At other times, Mrs. T has bizarre visual hallucinations. For example, she saw cherubs in the grocery store. These experiences leave her preoccupied, confused, and frightened, unable to perform such everyday tasks as cooking or playing the piano.

Schizophrenia is an extraordinary disorder. There have been various attempts to define the symptoms, but it has always been easier to identify schizophrenic behavior (such as bizarre hallucinations and disturbances of thought) than to define the term. The important point is that the symptoms of schizophrenia vary from case to case. It was proposed in 1913 that schizophrenia was characterized by a progressively deteriorating course with little chance of recovery. This was the dominant opinion through most of the twentieth century, but a consensus is emerging that this view is probably incorrect. Most patients appear to stay fairly stable after the first few years of the disease, with little evidence of a decline in functioning. The symptoms come and go, as in Mrs. T's case.

Numerous studies have looked at the gross morphology of the brain of schizophrenics, both in autopsied tissue and using magnetic resonance and computerized tomography scans. Most researchers agree that schizophrenics have brains that weigh less than normal and in which the ventricles are enlarged. There have been suggestions that schizophrenics have smaller frontal lobes, or at least reductions in the number of neurons in the frontal cortex.

■ **Learn more about higher brain functions** Search the Internet for *corpus callosum*, *pure word blindness*, *Phineas Gage*, and *split-brain patients.*

Glossary

Acetylcholine The neurotransmitter at cholinergic synapses, which in the peripheral nervous system causes cardiac inhibition, vasodilation, and gastrointestinal movements.

Action potential An electrical excitation of the neuronal membrane, giving rise to an electrical impulse that travels down the axon, providing the basic unit of communication of the nervous system.

Affect The conscious subjective aspect of feeling or emotion.

Afferent Toward the central nervous system.

Anencephalia A defect in brain development resulting in small or missing brain hemispheres.

Anomic aphasia A condition that is characterized by the inability to recall names of persons or things.

Anterograde amnesia Impairments of memory for events occurring after the onset of amnesia; inability to form new memories.

Aphasia Partial or total loss of the ability to articulate ideas or comprehend spoken and written language, resulting from damage to the brain caused by injury or disease.

Autonomic Acting or occurring involuntarily.

Axon A long, slender projection of a nerve cell that conducts electrical impulses away from the cell body.

Baroreflex The reflex of the body that controls blood pressure, triggered by receptors in blood vessels that sense an increase in blood pressure, which decreases heart rate and subsequently lowers blood pressure.

Bipolar neuron A nerve cell with two processes arising from opposite poles of the cell body.

Caudate nucleus A subsection of a part of the brain called the basal ganglia that is involved in the control of movement.

Cognition Mental functions such as the ability to think, reason, and remember.

Corticospinal tract Collection of nerve fibers that begins in the cerebral cortex and ends on motor neuron cells in the spinal cord to drive voluntary movements.

Dementia The loss of intellectual functions of sufficient severity to interfere with a person's daily functioning.

Dendrite A slender projection of a nerve cell, usually with branches. It conducts electrical signals from other cells into the cell body.

Dependence Being abnormally tolerant to something that is habit-forming.

Dermatology The medical specialty concerned with treating diseases of the skin, hair, and nails.

Diencephalon Region of the brain located above the brain stem and including the thalamus and hypothalamus.

Dopamine A neurotransmitter present in regions of the brain that regulate movement, emotion, motivation, and feelings of pleasure.

Dorsal Referring to the back or top side of an animal.

Dyslexia A reading disorder characterized by reading ability below he expected level given a child's age, school grade, and intelligence.

Efferent Away from the central nervous system.

Electrical potential Measure of the ability to create electricity; also known as voltage.

Free nerve endings Unspecialized receptors that are at the ends of nerves without the myelin sheath and are concerned with the sensation of pain and temperature.

Globus pallidus A group of cells deep in the brain that affects movement, balance, and walking. Acts as an intermediate relay system with the rest of the body to control complex movements.

Gray matter Brownish-gray nerve tissue of the brain and spinal cord, composed of nerve cell bodies, their dendrites, and supporting tissue.

Gustation Act or sensation of tasting.

Hippocampus The part of the brain that assists in memory by sorting and sending new bits of information to be stored in appropriate sections of the brain and recalling when necessary.

Homeostasis In medicine and biology, the inherent tendency in an organism to maintain physiological and psychological stability.

Hydrocephalus An accumulation of cerebrospinal fluid within the skull, causing dangerous expansion of the cerebral ventricles and, in infants, expansion of the skull itself.

Hypothalamus Small structure at the base of the brain that regulates many body functions, including appetite and body temperature.

Hypothyroidism Diminished production of thyroid hormone, leading to thyroid insufficiency, low metabolic rate, and weight gain.

Innervate To supply a body part, tissue, or organ with nerves.

Interneuron A nerve cell that only communicates with other neurons; the "in-between neuron."

Intravenous The administration of a drug or fluid directly into a vein.

Lateral Pertaining to the sides of a body.

Limbic system A circuit of midline structures circling the thalamus that plays a role in the control and production of emotional behavior.

Long-term memory Enduring memories about things, places, and events that last for over 30 seconds to years.

Long-term potentiation Long-lasting strengthening of the connection between two nerve cells.

Meissner's corpuscles Skin receptors that transduce sensations of light touch.

Mesencephalon The midbrain between the pons and the thalamus.

Metencephalon The rostral subdivision of the hindbrain during embryonic development. It is situated between the midbrain and the medulla oblongata. The adult derivative is the pons and the cerebellum.

Mood Temper, a characteristic state of feeling.

Motor neuron Nerve cell in the spinal cord that sends its axons to muscles to facilitate contraction.

Multipolar neuron A nerve cell with a single axon and many dendrites.

Myelencephalon The most posterior part of the brain stem, also called the medulla.

Myelin An insulating fatty layer that surrounds axons and speeds the conduction of electrical impulses along the axon.

Neural crest A cluster of cells found at each side of the neural tube. It gives rise to many of the cells of the nervous system.

Neural tube Embryonic structure that gives rise to the brain and spinal cord.

Neurotransmitter A chemical that transmits signals between nerve cells.

Node of Ranvier A regularly spaced gap in the myelin sheath around an axon. This gap exposes the axonal membrane to the surrounding fluid. Action potentials "jump" from node to node since the node is the only place where ion flow occurs.

Obsessive-compulsive disorder (OCD) Anxiety disorder characterized by intense, recurrent, unwanted thoughts and rituals that are beyond the person's control.

Optic chiasm The point of crossing of the optic nerves.

Pacinian corpuscles Pressure receptor located deep underneath the skin.

Panic An overwhelming feeling of fear and anxiety.

Pathology The scientific study of the nature of disease and its causes, processes, development, and consequences.

Post-traumatic stress disorder (PTSD) A debilitating condition that often follows a terrifying physical or emotional event, causing the person who survived the event to have persistent, frightening thoughts and memories, or flashbacks, of the ordeal.

Pseudounipolar neuron A nerve cell that appears to have a single process but actually has two processes branching out from a single one.

Psychosis A state of mind in which thinking becomes irrational or disturbed.

Putamen Structure in the middle of the brain that plays a role in movement.

Reflex An automatic, instinctive unlearned reaction to a stimulus.

Retrograde amnesia Inability to recall events before the actual onset of amnesia; loss of memories of past events.

Sensory neuron Cell of the nervous system responsible for converting external stimuli into electrical impulses that can be transmitted to the brain.

Short-term memory Sometimes referred to as "active" or "primary" memory, it stores a limited amount of information for a limited amount of time (about 30–45 seconds).

Social phobia A disorder that results in extreme anxiety in social situations. Those who suffer from social phobia experience intense and disabling self-consciousness in these situations.

Soma Body of the neuron that contains the nucleus.

Somatic Related to the body.

Spina bifida A congenital defect in which the spinal column is imperfectly closed so that part of the meninges or spinal cord protrudes, often resulting in hydrocephalus or other neurological disorders.

Substantia nigra A small area of the brain containing a cluster of black-pigmented nerve cells that contain dopamine. Loss of cells in this region leads to Parkinson's disease.

Subthalamic nuclei A cluster of cells located in the ventral part of the subthalamus. It is the driving nuclei of the basal ganglia. Dysfunction leads to exaggerated movements.

Synapse A specialized cellular junction through which the cells of the nervous system communicate with one another.

Telencephalon The anterior-most division of the neural tube, which forms the cerebral cortex and immediate subcortical structures.

Tight junction The closely associated area of two cells whose membranes bind together to form a single layer.

Tolerance A condition in which higher doses of a drug are needed to produce the same effect as during initial use.

Tumescence Resulting from the presence of excess blood or other fluids in the tissue.

Umami The fifth type of basic taste; it is the taste of substances such as glutamate and monosodium glutamate (MSG).

Vasoconstriction Reduction in the size of blood vessels leading to decrease in local blood flow.

Ventral Pertaining to the underside or belly of a body.

Visceral Relating to an internal organ such as the heart, liver, or kidney.

Wallerian degeneration Degradation of axons and their myelin sheaths originating from neuronal injury.

White matter Nervous tissue of the brain and spinal cord, consisting chiefly of myelinated nerve fibers.

Bibliography

Adam, G. *Visceral Perception.* New York: Plenum, 1998.

Agranoff, B.W., and M.D. Uhler. "Learning and memory." In Siegel, G.J., B.W. Agranoff, R.W. Albers, et al. (eds.), *Basic Neurochemistry,* 5th ed. New York: Raven Press, 1994.

Aldrich, M.S. "Narcolepsy." *New England Journal of Medicine* 323 (1990): 389–394.

Allheid, G.F., L. Heimer, R.C. Switzer. "Basal ganglia." In Paxinos, G. (ed.). *The Human Nervous System.* San Diego, CA: Academic Press, 1990.

American Psychiatric Association. *Diagnostic and Statistical Manual (DSM–IV),* 4th ed. Washington, DC: American Psychiatric Association, 1998.

Barchas, J.D., M.W. Hamblin, and R.C. Malenka. "Biochemical hypotheses of mood and anxiety disorders." In Siegel, G.J., B.W. Agranoff, R.W. Albers, et al. (eds.), *Basic Neurochemistry,* 5th ed. New York: Raven Press, 1994.

Barh, M., N.P. Rosman. "Cerebral malformations and neurocutaneous disorders." In Brandt, T., L.R. Caplan, J. Dichgans, et al. (eds.), *Neurological Disorders: Course and Treatment.* New York: Academic Press, 1996.

Benson, D.F., and E. Zaidel. *The Dual Brain: Hemispheric Specialization in Humans.* New York: Guilford Press, 1985.

Brooks, V.B. *The Neural Basis of Motor Control.* New York: Oxford University Press, 1986.

Cervero, F. "Mechanisms of visceral pain: past and present." In Gebhart, G.F. (ed.). *Visceral Pain.* Seattle, WA: IASP Press, 1995.

Copp, A.J., et al. "The embryonic development of mammalian neural tube defects." *Progress in Neurobiology* 35 (1990): 363.

Crelin, E.S. "Development of the nervous system." *CIBA Clinical Symposia* 26:2 (1974).

Damasio, A.R. "Aphasia." *New England Journal of Medicine* 326 (1992): 531.

Dronkers, N.F., S. Pinker, and A. Damasio. "Language and the aphasias." In Kandel, E.R., J.H. Schwartz, and T.M. Jessell (eds.), *Principles of Neuroscience,* 4th ed. New York: McGraw-Hill, 2000.

Dudai, Y. *The Neurobiology of Memory.* New York: Oxford University Press, 1989.

Elfvin, L.G., B. Lindh, and T. Hokfelt. "The chemical neuroanatomy of sympathetic ganglia." *Annual Review of Neuroscience* 16 (1993): 471–507.

Finger, T.E., and W.L. Silver. *Neurobiology of Taste and Smell.* New York: John Wiley & Sons, 1987.

Gardner, R.A., and B.T. Gardner. "Teaching sign language to a chimpanzee." *Science* 165 (1969): 664–672.

Goldman-Rakic, P.S., and L.D. Selemon. "New frontiers in basal ganglia research." *TINS* 13 (1990): 241.

Hartmann, E. *Dreams and Nightmares.* New York: Plenum, 1998.

Hauser, M. *The Evolution of Communication.* Cambridge, MA: The MIT Press, 1996.

Iversen, S., I. Kupfermann, and E.R. Kandel. "Emotional states and feelings." In Kandel, E.R., J.H. Schwartz, and T.M. Jessell (eds.), *Principles of Neuroscience,* 4th ed. New York: McGraw-Hill, 2000.

Jones, E.G., and W.M. Cowan. "Nervous tissue." In Weiss, L. (ed.). *Histology: Cell and Tissue Biology,* 5th ed. New York: Elsevier, 1983.

Kandel, E.R. "Cellular mechanisms of learning and the biological basis of individuality." In Kandel, E.R., J.H. Schwartz, and T.M. Jessell (eds.), *Principles of Neuroscience,* 4th ed. New York: McGraw-Hill, 2000.

Kandel, E.R. "Disorders of mood: depression, mania and anxiety disorders." In Kandel, E.R., J.H. Schwartz, and T.M. Jessell (eds.), *Principles of Neuroscience,* 4th ed. New York: McGraw-Hill, 2000.

Kandel, E.R. "The brain and behaviors." In Kandel, E.R., J.H. Schwartz, T.M. Jessell (eds.), *Principles of Neuroscience,* 4th ed. New York: McGraw-Hill, 2000.

Kandel, E.R., I. Kupfermann, and S. Iversen. "Learning and memory." In Kandel, E.R., J.H. Schwartz, and T.M. Jessell (eds.), *Principles of Neuroscience,* 4th ed. New York: McGraw-Hill, 2000.

Kolb, B., and I.Q. Whishaw. "Functional organization of the cortex." In Atkinson, R.C., G. Lindzey, and R.F. Thompson (eds.), *Fundamentals of Human Neuropsychology,* 4th ed. New York: W.H. Freeman, 1996.

Lemire, R.J., et al. *Normal and Abnormal Development of the Human Nervous System.* New York: Harper & Row, 1975.

Lesson, T.S., C.R. Lesson, and A.A. Paparo. *Text/Atlas of Histology.* Philadelphia: Saunders, 1988.

Loewy, A.D., and K.M. Spyer (eds.), *Central Regulation of Autonomic Function.* New York: Oxford University Press, 1990.

Mahowald, M., and C. Schenck. "REM sleep behaviors disorder." In Kryger, M.H., T. Roth, and W.C. Dement (eds.), *Principles and Practice of Sleep Medicine,* 2nd ed. Philadelphia: Saunders, 1994.

McMahon, S., and M. Koltzenburg (eds.), *The Textbook of Pain,* 5th ed. New York: Churchill & Livingstone, 2005.

Michels, R. (ed.). *Psychiatry.* Philadelphia: Lippincott, 1992.

Nolte, J. *The Human Brain,* 3rd ed. St. Louis, MO: Mosby, 1993.

Penfield, W., and L. Roberts. *Speech and Brain Mechanisms.* Princeton, NJ: Princeton University Press, 1959.

Rechtschaffen, A., and J. Siegel. "Sleep and dreaming." In Kandel, E.R., J.H. Schwartz, and T.M. Jessell (eds.), *Principles of Neuroscience,* 4th ed. New York: McGraw-Hill, 2000.

Roth, T., and T. Roehrs. "Disorders of sleep and wakefulness." In Kandel, E.R., J.H. Schwartz, and T.M. Jessell (eds.), *Principles of Neuroscience,* 4th ed. New York: McGraw-Hill, 2000.

Schuri, U., B.A. Wilson, J.R. Hodges. "Memory Disorders." In Brandt, T., L.R. Caplan, J. Dichgans, et al. (eds.), *Neurological Disorders: Course and Treatment.* San Diego, CA: Academic Press, 1996.

Shaywitz, S.E. "Dyslexia." *New England Journal of Medicine* 338 (1998): 307–312.

Squire, L.R. "Memory and the hippocampus: A synthesis from findings with rats, monkeys, and humans." *Psychological Review* 99 (1992): 195–231.

Van De Graff, K.M., and S.I. Fox. *Concepts of Human Anatomy and Physiology,* 3rd ed. Dubuque, Iowa: WCB, 1992.

Villee, C.A., E.P. Solomon, C.E. Martin, et al. (eds.), *Biology,* 2nd ed. Philadelphia: Saunders, 1989.

Weiner, W.J., and A.E Lang. *Movement Disorders: A Comprehensive Survey,* New York: Futura Publishing, 1989.

Further Reading

Barondes, S.H. *Molecules and Mental Illness.* New York: Scientific American Library, 1993.

Churchland, P.M. *The Engine of Reason, the Seat of the Soul.* Cambridge, MA: MIT Press, 1996.

Czener, T.B. *What Makes You Tick? The Brain in Plain English.* New York: Wiley, 2001.

Fleischmann, J. *Phineas Gage: A Gruesome but True Story About Brain Science.* Boston: Houghton Mifflin, 2002.

Higbee, K.L. *Your Memory: How It Works and How to Improve It.* New York: Marlowe and Company, 2001.

Horne, J. *Why We Sleep: The Functions of Sleep in Humans and Other Mammals*: New York: Oxford University Press, 1988.

Paxinos, G. *The Human Nervous System.* San Diego, CA: Academic Press, 1990.

Porter, R. *Madness: A Brief History.* New York: Oxford University Press, 2003.

Schacter, D. *Searching for Memory: The Brain, the Mind, and the Past,* 4th ed. New York: HarperCollins/Basic Books, 1994.

Squire, L., and E.R. Kandel. *Memory: From Mind to Molecules.* New York: Scientific American Library, 2000.

Stafford T., and M. Webb. *Mind Hacks: Tips and Tricks for Using Your Brain.* Cambridge: O'Reilly Media Inc., 2004.

Web Sites

Aphasia
http://www.aphasia.org

Autonomic Dysreflexia
http://calder.med.miami.edu/pointis/automatic.html

Congenital Insensitivity to Pain
http://helium.vancouver.wsu.edu/~woodc/CIPA.html

Drug Abuse
http://www.nida.nih.gov

Hydrocephalus Information
http://www.hydroassoc.org

Learning Disabilities
http://www.ldonline.org

Mental Disorders
http://www.mentalhelp.net

National Multiple Sclerosis Society
http://www.nationalmssociety.org

Parkinson's Disease
http://www.michaeljfox.org

Sleep Apnea
http://www.sleepapnea.org

Picture Credits

2: Infobase Publishing
3: Infobase Publishing
10: Infobase Publishing
13: Infobase Publishing
14: Infobase Publishing
21: Infobase Publishing
25: Infobase Publishing
27: Infobase Publishing
30: Infobase Publishing
33: Infobase Publishing
34: Infobase Publishing
40: Infobase Publishing
42: Infobase Publishing
47: Infobase Publishing
49: Infobase Publishing
56: © Anna Clopet/CORBIS
59: Infobase Publishing
64: Infobase Publishing
66: Neil Borden/Photo Researchers, Inc.
68: Annabella Bluesky/Photo Researchers, Inc.
72: Infobase Publishing
75: WDCN/Univ. College London/Photo Researchers, Inc.
81: Infobase Publishing
85: The Granger Collection, New York

Index

About the Author

Louis Vera-Portocarrero began his academic training at Prairie View A&M University (B.S., Biology), and he then studied at the University of Texas Medical Branch (Ph.D.) and the University of Arizona (postdoctoral training). He holds a research associate position in the Department of Pharmacology, College of Medicine, at the University of Arizona, where his time is devoted almost exclusively to research to understand chronic pain–processing mechanisms of the spinal cord and brain. He has published numerous peer-reviewed articles in the primary scientific literature, and he has taught chemistry, biology, calculus, and neuroscience. He is a member of the Society for Neuroscience, American Pain Society, and the International Association for the Study of Pain. He lives in Tucson, Arizona.

About the Editor

Eric H. Chudler, Ph.D., is a research neuroscientist who has investigated the brain mechanisms of pain and nociception since 1978. Dr. Chudler received his Ph.D. from the Department of Psychology at the University of Washington in Seattle. He has worked at the National Institutes of Health and directed a laboratory in the neurosurgery department at Massachusetts General Hospital. Between 1991 and 2006, Dr. Chudler was a faculty member in the Department of Anesthesiology at the University of Washington. He is currently a research associate professor in the University of Washington Department of Bioengineering and director of education and outreach at University of Washington Engineered Biomaterials. Dr. Chudler's research interests focus on how the cerebral cortex and basal ganglia process information related to pain. He has also worked with other neuroscientists and teachers to develop educational materials to help students learn about the brain.